TRANSFORMED

How God Changes Us

Be transformed by the renewing of your mind . . .

ROMANS 12:2

Taught by Rick Warren

Transformed: How God Changes Us
Small Group Study Guide
Edition 1.0

Copyright © 2014 Saddleback Church

ISBN: 978-1-4228-0254-0

Daily Devotions written by Johnny Baker, Kathy Camarillo, Jamin Goggin, Tommy Hilliker, Dave Holden, Tom Holladay, Bill Mugford, Ruben Meulenberg, Buddy Owens

Requests for information should be addressed to:
Saddleback Resources
29801 Santa Margarita Pkwy
Rancho Santa Margarita, CA 92688

Editorial context by Buddy Owens
Designed by Emily Okada
Fonts used: Futura Std and Georgia

Printed and bound in China

CONTENTS

TRANSFORMED

"BE TRANSFORMED BY THE RENEWING OF YOUR MIND." ROMANS 12:2 NIV

The only way to truly change your life is to change the way you think. That's why the Bible says in our theme verse, *"Do not conform any longer to the pattern of this world, but be transformed by the renewing of your mind."* (Romans 12:2 NIV)

What is the difference between "conforming" and "transforming?" According to the dictionary, to conform means to "make or become the same" or "to behave in a conventional way by accepting without question the customs, traditions and prevailing opinions of others." In other words, to conform is to fit into somebody else's mold; it's to do things the way everybody else does.

On the other hand, to transform means to "change the condition, function, nature, character or personality" of something.

> **CONFORMING** has to do with BEHAVIOR.
> **TRANSFORMING** has to do with CHARACTER.
> **CONFORMING** is FROM THE OUTSIDE IN.
> **TRANSFORMING** is FROM THE INSIDE OUT.

Conforming is something we do to ourselves. Transforming is something God does to us. And he transforms us by renewing our minds. You see, God doesn't just want to change your behavior. He wants to change the way you think. The Bible says, *"As a man thinks in his heart, so is he."* (Proverbs 23:7 NKJV) **Your thoughts control your actions.** So if you want to change the way you act, you must start by changing the way you think. If you want to be like Christ, you must learn to think like Christ.

Over the next seven weeks, we are going to study the transforming power of Jesus Christ. Specifically, we'll look at God's plan to transform you in seven key areas of your life: your **spiritual health, physical health, mental health, emotional health, relational health, financial health, and your vocational health**. We will allow God's Word to renew our minds and change the way we think: about God, about ourselves, about our relationships, our finances, our careers—about everything. And when you learn to think differently you will begin to live differently. As you learn to think God's way, you will begin to live God's way.

Transformation is about more than just putting information in your head. It's about living out what God is working in you. The Bible says *"Be doers of the Word, and not hearers only"* (James 1:22 NKJV). To help you apply what you are learning, we strongly encourage you to set a three month goal for each of the key areas of your life. **Goals turn intentions into actions.** Without a specific goal in mind, you might not get around to applying God's truth to your life. So we have provided instruction in the **Putting It into Practice** section of each session to help you set a three month goal for the key area you are studying.

Be sure your goal is a **SMART** goal: **Specific, Measurable, Attainable, Relevant,** and **Time-bound.** For example, don't just say, "I want to grow spiritually," or "I want to lose weight." Those are not **SMART goals**. They're too general. A **SMART goal** for your spiritual health might be, "I will memorize Romans 12 in the next ninety days," or "I will spend fifteen minutes in a quiet time every morning for the next three months." A **SMART goal** for your physical health might be "I will lose twenty pounds in the next ninety days." Those are **SMART goals**: they are based on a specific action that is measurable and doable, they relate to the particular area of health you are studying, and they have a deadline.

Once you have set your goal, transfer that goal to the **My Three-Month Goals** list on pages vi to vii of this study guide so that you can have them all in one place for easy reference.

We have also included **seven daily devotions** that relate to the area of health you are focusing on during each week, along with journal pages for each day. Each journal page gives you four prompts:

- **What did you hear?** *What did God say to you as you read the devotion for the day?*
- **What do you think?** *What does it mean to you, how does it apply to your life, and what difference does it make to you?*
- **What will you do?** *What action step will you take? How will you think differently? How will you live differently?*
- **Now You Pray** . . . *This is where you put your thoughts into prayer. It could be a prayer of gratitude or praise. It could be a prayer of confession or a request for God's help. It's up to you. But take a minute each day to write a prayer response to what you read in the devotion.*

Are you ready to be transformed? Then let's begin.

HOW TO USE THIS WORKBOOK

A brief explanation of the features of this workbook.

MY THREE-MONTH GOALS

Each week you will set a personal goal for the area of health you are studying with your group. Transfer each goal to the **My Three-Month Goals** page so you can have them all in one place.

WEEKEND SERMON NOTES

You can use this page to take notes on your pastor's sermon each weekend.

SMALL GROUP STUDY

 CHECKING IN: Open each meeting by briefly discussing a question or two that will help focus everyone's attention on the subject of the lesson.

MEMORY VERSE: Each week you will find a key Bible verse for your group to memorize together. If someone in the group has a different translation, ask them to read it aloud so the group can get a bigger picture of the meaning of the passage.

VIDEO LESSON: There is a video lesson for the group to watch together each week. Fill in the blanks in the lesson outlines as you watch the video and be sure to refer back to these outlines during your discussion time.

DISCOVERY QUESTIONS: Each video segment is complemented by several questions for group discussion. Please don't feel pressured to discuss every single question. There is no reason to rush through the answers. Give everyone ample opportunity to share their thoughts. If you don't get through all of the discussion questions, that's okay.

 PUTTING IT INTO PRACTICE: Each week you will be challenged to commit to one goal in each of the seven key areas of this study. Be sure to transfer these goals to the **My Three-Month Goals** page on page vi to vii of the workbook.

 PRAYER DIRECTION: At the end of each session you will find suggestions for your group prayer time. Praying together is one of the greatest privileges of small group life. Please don't take it for granted.

 DIVING DEEPER: This section includes suggestions for books, studies, and other resources for personal and group use.

DAILY DEVOTIONS AND JOURNAL PAGES

There are seven daily devotions and seven journal pages at the end of each session in your study guide. Use these for your daily quiet times throughout the week.

SMALL GROUP RESOURCES

There are additional small group resources, such as Group Guidelines, Helps for Hosts, Prayer and Praise Reports, etc., in the back of this study guide.

A TIP FOR THE HOST

The study guide material is meant to be your servant, not your master. The point is not to race through the sessions; the point is to take time to let God work in your lives. Nor is it necessary to "go around the circle" before you move on to the next question. Give people the freedom to speak, but don't insist on it. Your group will enjoy deeper, more open sharing and discussion if people don't feel pressured to speak up.

MY THREE-MONTH GOALS

MY THREE-MONTH SPIRITUAL HEALTH **GOAL**

MY THREE-MONTH PHYSICAL HEALTH **GOAL**

MY THREE-MONTH MENTAL HEALTH **GOAL**

MY THREE-MONTH EMOTIONAL HEALTH **GOAL**

MY THREE-MONTH RELATIONAL HEALTH **GOAL**

MY THREE-MONTH FINANCIAL HEALTH **GOAL**

MY THREE-MONTH VOCATIONAL HEALTH **GOAL**

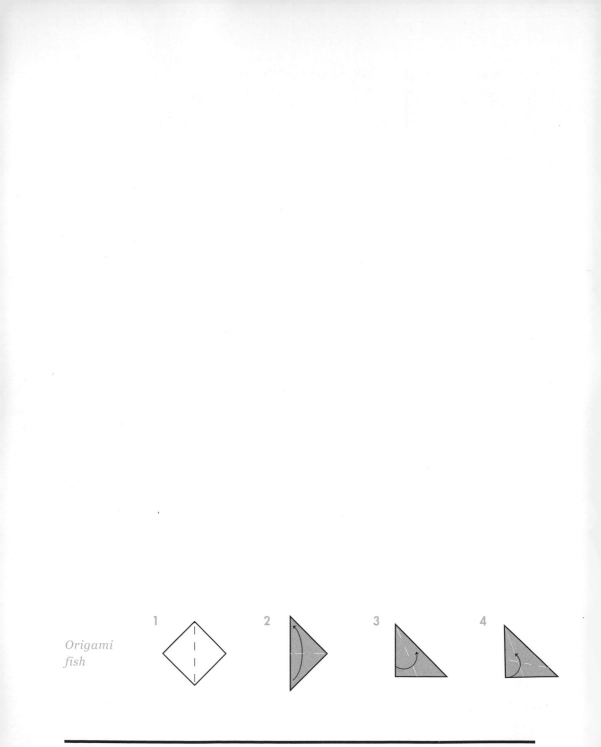

*Origami
fish*

1

2

3

4

TRANSFORMED

IN MY SPIRITUAL

HEALTH

SESSION 1

WEEKEND SERMON NOTES

4

SESSION 1
TRANSFORMED IN MY SPIRITUAL HEALTH

◇ CHECKING IN

- If this is your first time to meet as a group, or if you have any new group members, be sure to **introduce yourselves**.

- Before you begin this study, we recommend that you review the **Small Group Guidelines** on page 216 of this workbook as a group.

- Share with the group what you hope to get out of this small group series.

◇ MEMORY VERSE

Anyone who belongs to Christ has become a new person.
The old life is gone; a new life has begun!

2 CORINTHIANS 5:17 (NLT)

◇ WATCH THE VIDEO LESSON NOW AND FOLLOW ALONG IN YOUR OUTLINE.

→

◈ TRANSFORMED IN MY SPIRITUAL HEALTH
SEVEN HABITS FOR SPIRITUAL HEALTH

1. I must _____ supremely.

    "If you want to be my follower you must love me more than your own father and mother, wife and children, brothers and sisters—yes, more than your own life. Otherwise, you cannot be my disciple."

    LUKE 14:26 (NLT)

    Spiritual health is measured by _____ .

    "The most important commandment is this . . . you must love the Lord your God with all your heart, [passionately], all your soul, [willfully], all your mind, [thoughtfully], and all your strength [practically—live like you love him]."

    MARK 12:29–30 (NLT)

2. I must _____ .

    Blessed is the man who listens to me, watching daily at my doors, waiting at my doorway.

    PROVERBS 8:34 (NIV)

3. I must _____ and _____ his Word.

    Blessed is the man . . . [whose] delight is in the law of the Lord, and on his law he meditates day and night. He is like a tree planted by streams of water, which yields its fruit in season and whose leaf does not wither. Whatever he does prospers.

    PSALM 1:1–3 (NIV)

    "You are my friends if you do what I command."

    JOHN 15:14 (NIV)

The man who looks intently into the perfect law that gives freedom, and continues to do this, not forgetting what he has heard, but doing it—he will be blessed in what he does.

JAMES 1:25 (NIV)

4. I must _____ my income.

"Bring the whole tithe into the storehouse, that there may be food in my house. Test me in this," says the Lord Almighty, "and see if I will not throw open the floodgates of heaven and pour out so much blessing that you will not have room enough for it."

MALACHI 3:10 (NIV)

You cannot out-give God!

5. I must learn to _____ .

"If you have love for one another, then everyone will know that you are my disciples."

JOHN 13:35 (TEV)

If someone says, "I love God," but hates a Christian brother or sister, that person is a liar; for if we don't love people we can see, how can we love God, whom we have not seen?

1 JOHN 4:20 (NLT)

Spiritual growth happens in _____ .

6. I must _____ .

"For even I, the Son of Man, came here not to be served but to serve others, and to give my life as a ransom for many."

MARK 10:45 (NLT)

7. I must pass on the _____ .

> *Take the teachings that you heard me proclaim in the presence of many*
> *witnesses, and entrust them to reliable people, who will be able to teach*
> *others also.*

2 TIMOTHY 2:2 (TEV)

You're going to go to heaven because somebody told you about **Jesus Christ**. And somebody told the somebody who told you. And somebody told the somebody who told the somebody who told you. Is the chain going to break with you? Is anybody going to be in heaven because of you? If you don't tell somebody, then who is going to tell them? Jesus says to be a disciple you must pass on the **Good News**.

> *"Go and make disciples of all the nations, baptizing them in the name of the*
> *Father and the Son and the Holy Spirit. Teach these new disciples to obey all the*
> *commands I have given you. And be sure of this: I am with you always, even to*
> *the end of the age."*

MATTHEW 28:19–20 (NLT)

8

◇ DISCOVERY QUESTIONS
(PICK AT LEAST ONE OR TWO)

- What seems to get in the way of your **spiritual growth**?

- In the video you learned about the importance of a **daily time with God**. How do you have a **daily time with God**? What is your normal routine? What typically interferes with your **time with God**?

- Why is being in a small group and serving others so important to your **spiritual growth**? What can you learn through relationships that you can't learn on your own?

- In the video Pastor Rick said, **"Spiritual growth is not automatic. It is a choice."** In what ways have you chosen to grow spiritually? What has been most effective in helping you grow?

◈ PUTTING IT INTO PRACTICE

In this session we discussed the seven habits that help us grow spiritually. **Which of these habits do you need to work on the most? What is one thing you can do to begin to make that habit a reality in your daily life in the next three months?** Talk about this with your group and share ideas with each other.

Settle on one thing you will do and make a **three-month goal** to grow in this area of spiritual health. Write your goal in the space below.

MY THREE-MONTH SPIRITUAL HEALTH **GOAL**

10

When it comes to setting goals, it is important that you make a plan and then check your progress on a regular basis. Goals that are not written down and set in motion are just ideas, and we rarely feel any commitment to following through on all of our ideas. To help you reach your goals, we have provided the **My Three-Month Goals** list on page vi of this workbook. Visit this page each week and add one goal for each of the seven areas we will cover in this study. The purpose of the **My Three-Month Goals** list is to help you begin to put into practice the things you are learning in this study. We recommend that you review the **My Three-Month Goals** page on a regular basis to remind yourself of your goals and to track your progress. You may even want to set a time in the future as a group to share how each group member is doing with their goals and celebrate what God is doing in each of your lives.

For this session, transfer your **Three-Month Spiritual Health Goal** to the **My Three-Month Goals** list on pages vi to vii.

◈ PRAYER DIRECTION

One way we can show our love for one another is by committing to pray for one another. Take some time as a group to share your prayer requests. Be sure to record everyone's requests on the **Small Group Prayer and Praise Report** on page 218.

◈ DIVING DEEPER

WANT TO GO DEEPER IN YOUR SPIRITUAL HEALTH?

FOR YOU

- Read the **daily devotions** for days 1—7 in your workbook.

- Read the **Memory Verse** on page 5 every day this week as part of your quiet time. See if you can have it memorized before your next group meeting.

- Read *The Purpose Driven Life* by Pastor Rick Warren. Since its release, this book has become "the best-selling non-fiction hardback book in history," according to Publishers Weekly. It will help you understand what spiritual health is all about and find the answers to three of life's most important questions:

  1. The Question of **Existence**: *Why am I alive?*

  2. The Question of **Significance**: *Does my life matter?*

  3. The Question of **Purpose**: *What on earth am I here for?*

  Living out the purpose you were created for moves you beyond mere survival and success to a life of significance—the life you were meant to live. Available at **www.saddlebackresources.com**.

- Get a **spiritual check-up**. Most people want to live healthy, balanced lives. A regular medical checkup is a good way to measure physical health and spot potential problems. In the same way, a spiritual checkup is vital to your spiritual well-being. **The Purpose Driven Spiritual Health Assessment** will give you a quick snapshot of your spiritual health. Take 3–4 minutes alone to complete the **Purpose Driven Spiritual Health Assessment**, found on page 220 of this workbook. After answering the questions, tally your results. Then pair up with another person and briefly share one purpose that is going well and one that needs a little work.

FOR THE GROUP

Consider for your next group study, *What On Earth Am I Here For?* by Rick Warren. Based on his best-selling book, *The Purpose Driven Life*, this DVD and study guide will take participants on a journey of discovery to answer life's most fundamental question: "What on earth am I here for?" Available at **www.saddlebackresources.com**.

EXPANDED PURPOSE DRIVEN LIFE BOOK

This book has transformed millions of lives. *Are you ready for a change?*

WHAT ON EARTH AM I HERE FOR STARTER PACK

Six sessions on why you were created, how to discover your identity, your meaning, purpose, significance, and your destiny

SADDLEBACKRESOURCES.COM

TRANSFORMED IN MY SPIRITUAL HEALTH
DAY 1

For God so loved the world that he gave his one and only Son, that whoever believes in him shall not perish but have eternal life.

JOHN 3:16 (NIV)

This is arguably the greatest verse in the entire Bible. There's a reason it has earned a spot on the bottom of fast food soft drink cups and on signs behind goal posts at football games. Why? Because it is Christianity in a nutshell. It simply and clearly tells us the Good News of Jesus Christ in four points.

God is passionate about you. This verse says, *"God so loved the world."* You are part of the world. God loves you. His love isn't detached and impersonal. It is passionate. Do you know God loves you? He does.

He shows that love by his gift. That's the second point this verse tells us about God, *". . . that he gave his one and only Son."* God's love for you cost him more than we could ever measure. He gave you Jesus. He gave you Jesus to pay for your sins and to provide a bridge between you and God.

The third point we learn from John 3:16 is God's proposal to us, *"That whoever believes in him . . ."* We all have the opportunity to turn to Jesus. All it takes is belief. We don't have to earn God's love, all we have to do is accept his love in Jesus Christ.

When we do that we gain the fourth point from this verse, God's promise; *". . . shall not perish; but have eternal life."* What a deal! God loves you so much that he gave you Jesus. When you accept his proposal to believe in Christ, you gain the promise of eternal life. That is Good News.

If you haven't yet accepted God's proposal, do it today. If you have, live today in light of this verse. **God loves you, he gave you Jesus, and promises you eternal life.** That is what spiritual health is all about.

What did you hear?

_____
_____
_____
_____
_____

What do you think?

_____
_____
_____
_____
_____
_____

What will you do?

_____
_____
_____
_____
_____

Now talk to God . . .

_____
_____
_____
_____
_____

> *Yet to all who received him, to those who believed in his name,*
> *he gave the right to become children of God—children born*
> *not of natural descent, nor of human decision or a husband's*
> *will, but born of God.*

JOHN 1:12–13 (NIV)

We are God's children. When we believe in Jesus Christ we are brought near to God the Father. So near in fact that he calls us his sons and daughters. We are a part of his family now. Fully received, fully loved, and fully accepted.

What does this mean? It means we get to share in the very same relationship of love and intimacy that Jesus shared with the Father. Romans 8:15 (NIV) tells us, *"The Spirit you received does not make you slaves, so that you live in fear again; rather, the Spirit you received brought about your adoption to sonship. And by him we cry, 'Abba, Father.'"*

We should recognize this cry of, *"Abba, Father."* We have heard it before on the lips of Jesus as he prayed in the Garden of Gethsemane. Jesus cried out, *"Abba, Father ... everything is possible for you"* (Mark 14:36a NIV). Incredibly, we address God as "Abba, Father" just as Jesus does. We talk to God like Jesus does. **He has granted us full access** (Ephesians 2:18). No constraints, no caveats, no limitations. We are received. We are accepted. We belong. So much so, that we can boldly pray, "Abba, Father," along with Jesus. We share in the relational intimacy, love, and bond that the Father and Son have known for all eternity.

Jesus, the divine Son by nature, has invited you, by grace, to participate in his life of love with the Father. This is how much you have been received in his family. This is how much you belong. This is how much your identity is secured. God the Father has welcomed you into his house. In fact, as you cry out "Abba, Father," he says back, "My beloved child." **The Creator of the universe cherishes you and delights in you.**

What did you hear?

_____
_____
_____
_____
_____
_____

What do you think?

_____
_____
_____
_____
_____
_____
_____

What will you do?

_____
_____
_____
_____
_____
_____

Now talk to God . . .

_____
_____
_____
_____
_____

17

SPIRITUAL **HEALTH**

TRANSFORMED IN MY SPIRITUAL HEALTH
DAY 3

Ye are of God, little children, and have overcome them: because greater is he that is in you, than he that is in the world.

1 JOHN 4:4 (KJV)

God's Spirit is the power inside every fully devoted follower of Jesus Christ. Jesus promised every disciple, *"I will ask the Father, and he will give you another Advocate to help you and be with you forever—the Spirit of truth. . . [who] lives with you and will be in you,"* (John 14:16–17 NIV). But what does the Holy Spirit do for us?

The Holy Spirit helps us learn and apply God's truth to life: *"The Holy Spirit, whom the Father will send in my [Jesus'] name, will teach you all things and will remind you of everything I have said to you"* (John 14:26 NIV).

The Holy Spirit builds our character through crisis: *"We know that suffering produces perseverance; perseverance, character; and character, hope. And hope does not put us to shame, because God's love has been poured out into our hearts through the Holy Spirit, who has been given to us"* (Romans 5:3–5 NIV).

The Holy Spirit enables us to be more like Jesus: *"But the fruit of the Spirit is love, joy, peace, patience, kindness, goodness, faithfulness, gentleness and self-control"* (Galatians 5:22–23 NIV).

The Holy Spirit gives us power to speak the Good News of Jesus: *"But you will receive power when the Holy Spirit comes on you; and you will be my witnesses in Jerusalem, and in all Judea and Samaria, and to the ends of the earth"* (Acts 1:8 NIV).

The Holy Spirit equips us for ministry: *"There are different kinds of gifts, but the same Spirit distributes them. There are different kinds of service, but the same Lord. There are different kinds of working, but in all of them and in everyone it is the same God at work"* (1 Corinthians 12:4–6 NIV).

When we are filled with the Spirit, God's power, peace, presence and purpose are ours. We have stability under stress. We don't cave in, because, *"Greater is he that is in us, than he that is in the world."*

DAILY DEVOTIONS: DAY 3

What did you hear?

_____
_____
_____
_____
_____

What do you think?

_____
_____
_____
_____
_____

What will you do?

_____
_____
_____
_____
_____

Now talk to God . . .

_____
_____
_____
_____
_____

Anyone who belongs to Christ has become a new person.
The old life is gone; a new life has begun!

2 CORINTHIANS 5:17 (NLT)

When you come to Jesus Christ, it's like he writes everything you've ever done wrong on a big blackboard and then says, "We're just going to erase all that. We're going to start over. **You're going to get a fresh new start.**" It's not just turning over a new leaf, but getting a totally new life. You become a new person. Jesus gives you a new spiritual identity.

Here's the blunt truth of why this is so important. **Every time you sin, it damages your dignity.** When you break God's principles, you don't just hurt other people and God, you hurt yourself. Sin splits your soul. Every time you sin, it replaces a little bit of self-respect with a little bit of shame. This shame begins to pile up in your life and you begin to try to push it out of the way by staying busy or playing sports or getting drunk or having parties or whatever.

Jesus Christ is in the dignity restoring business. He doesn't just ignore your sin, he wipes it out and makes you a **new person** in his sight.

Hear this carefully. Because you are in Christ, it doesn't matter what you've done. It doesn't matter who you've done it with. It doesn't matter how long you've done it. It doesn't matter where you've been. What matters is what direction your feet are headed today. God says your past is history, your life has sanctity, and your identity has dignity because Jesus died for you. **When you trust Christ, he gives you a brand new identity and makes all things new!**

What did you hear?

_____
_____
_____
_____
_____
_____

What do you think?

_____
_____
_____
_____
_____
_____

What will you do?

_____
_____
_____
_____
_____
_____

Now talk to God . . .

_____
_____
_____
_____
_____
_____

SPIRITUAL **HEALTH**

TRANSFORMED IN MY SPIRITUAL HEALTH
DAY 5

The temptations in your life are no different from what others experience. And God is faithful. He will not allow the temptation to be more than you can stand. When you are tempted, he will show you a way out so that you can endure.

1 CORINTHIANS 10:13 (NLT)

Have you ever been so tempted to do something that you felt it was inevitable? Maybe a situation presented itself in such a way that something you knew was wrong felt very right. Or, you may have felt such overwhelming temptation that resistance seemed impossible. The truth is, we are all going to face temptation, probably every day.

Will we tell the truth when given the chance to lie and make ourselves look better? Will we be honest about the $20 bill we found on the ground? Will we give in to the habit that seems like it will never let us go, or will we seek help? We will all be tempted, but there's good news: **we don't have to give in**.

Today's verse promises that any time we are tempted, **God will provide a way out**. The problem too often is that when faced with temptation we forget to look for God's escape route. The way out may be to call a friend who can keep you accountable. It may be to memorize Bible verses to call to mind in the time of temptation. It may be to get up and walk—or run—out of a tempting situation. The key is to be aware of the way out that God gives you.

Today when you are tempted, stop for a moment and look around. Ask God where the escape route is, then choose to follow it.

What did you hear?

_____
_____
_____
_____
_____

What do you think?

_____
_____
_____
_____
_____

What will you do?

_____
_____
_____
_____
_____

Now talk to God . . .

_____
_____
_____
_____
_____

TRANSFORMED IN MY SPIRITUAL HEALTH
DAY 6

If we confess our sins, he is faithful and just and will forgive us our sins and purify us from all unrighteousness.

1 JOHN 1:9 (NIV)

Do people have to tell you things over and over and over again? It's as if somehow they don't think you are listening or taking them seriously . . . Hmmmmmm. My dad used to tell me, "Keep the engine oil clean in your cars and they will run forever!" That's great and true advice. When dirt gets in the oil it starts to wear out all the parts. It slows the car down. Soon, it can grind to a halt as it overheats and melts down in the middle of a busy freeway.

It was not uncommon for him to follow up a couple of months later by asking, "Hey! Are you keeping your oil clean? If you do it now you won't suffer later! It's easy to do—why not just get it done." I knew it was the right thing to do . . . but, I'm sure you can figure out the rest of the story. I can't tell you how many times I have regretted not keeping that oil clean and pure. It cost me plenty over time.

Sometimes we just don't listen. A case in point: When John the Apostle wrote today's verse he must have been well aware that many had forgotten this fundamental truth. Maybe you have too.

"Think of this," he says: **"1. Confess and your sins will be forgiven. 2. Confess and you will be renewed and made pure before God."** How is all of this possible? Because God is faithful. You can count on him at all times. Because he is just. That means he has every right and the authority to cancel out every debt your sinfulness has cost you, now and forever.

So, if you feel dirty . . . **confess**. If you feel worn out . . . **confess**. If you feel like you're on the verge of a meltdown on the freeway of life . . . **confess**. If you want to experience the blessing and hand of God on your life, **confess**. And God will take care of everything else.

DAILY DEVOTIONS: DAY 6

What did you hear?

_____
_____
_____
_____
_____

What do you think?

_____
_____
_____
_____
_____
_____

What will you do?

_____
_____
_____
_____
_____

Now talk to God . . .

_____
_____
_____
_____
_____

Who shall separate us from the love of Christ? Shall trouble or hardship or persecution or famine or nakedness or danger or sword? . . . No, in all these things we are more than conquerors through him who loved us. For I am convinced that neither death nor life, neither angels nor demons, neither the present nor the future, nor any powers, neither height nor depth, nor anything else in all creation, will be able to separate us from the love of God that is in Christ Jesus our Lord.

ROMANS 8:35–39 (NIV)

This challenging, comforting passage assures us of God's profound love for us as his children. And it's a promise for you if you have ever wondered, **"If God loves me, why do I suffer?"**

This text is challenging because it describes our Christian ancestors being persecuted, suffering separation from families, friends, livelihoods, homes, possessions—even life itself. Yet Paul comforts them and us, assuring all that **nothing can ever rip us from the loving embrace of God!**

The passage is also challenging because those suffering are identified as God's children: *"For those who are led by the Spirit of God are the children of God . . . And by him we cry, 'Abba, Father' . . . We are children . . . heirs of God and co-heirs with Christ . . . We share in* [Christ's] *sufferings in order that we may also share in his glory"* (Romans 8:14–17 NIV). God's loving, intimate relationship to his children is not diminished, but actually strengthened in suffering.

Suffering doesn't mean we are unloved by God, or that we have displeased or disappointed him. Remember, Jesus encourages those he loves, *"I have told you these things, so that in me you may have peace. In this world you will have trouble. But take heart! I have overcome the world"* (John 16:33 NIV).

DAILY DEVOTIONS: DAY 7

When we see that suffering is part of the human journey with our heavenly Father, we ask, "Can you imagine going through suffering without him?" And we believe his amazing promise, *"We know that in all things God works for the good of those who love him, who have been called according to his purpose"* (Romans 8:28 NIV).

What did you hear?

What do you think?

27

What will you do?

Now talk to God . . .

NOTES

NOTES

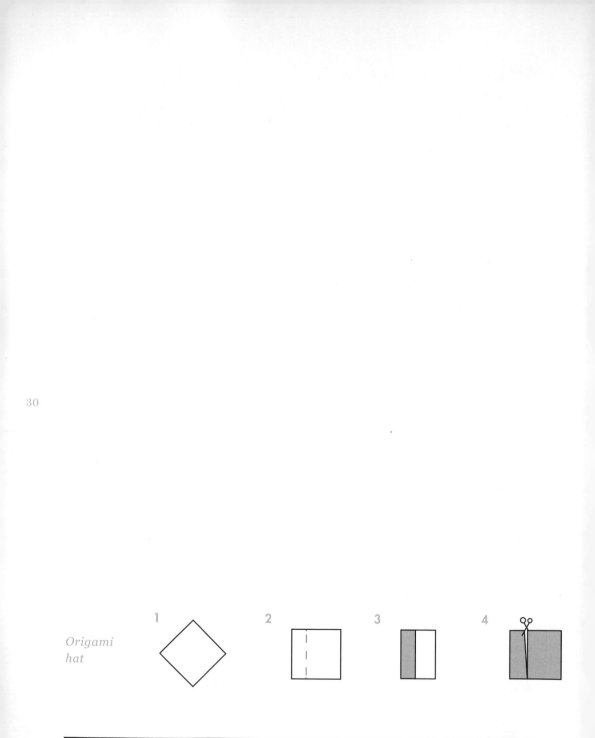

30

*Origami
hat*

1

2

3

4

SESSION 2

TRANSFORMED IN MY PHYSICAL HEALTH

SESSION 2

WEEKEND SERMON NOTES

SESSION 2

SESSION 2
TRANSFORMED IN MY PHYSICAL HEALTH

◈ CHECKING IN

- Which of the seven spiritual health verses from your devotional reading this past week was **the most meaningful to you?**

- What impact do you think your **physical health** has on your **spiritual health**?

◈ MEMORY VERSE

Do you not know that your body is a temple of the Holy Spirit, who is in you, whom you have received from God? You are not your own; you were bought at a price. Therefore honor God with your body.

1 CORINTHIANS 6:19–20 (NIV)

◈ WATCH THE VIDEO LESSON NOW AND FOLLOW ALONG IN YOUR OUTLINE.

→

◈ TRANSFORMED IN MY PHYSICAL HEALTH

I pray that you may enjoy good health and that all may go well with you, even as your soul is getting along well.

3 JOHN 1:2 (NIV)

God wants us to take care of our bodies, not only because that's where we live, but also because that's where *he* lives. **Physical health is a spiritual discipline.**

"Everything is permissible for me" – but not everything is beneficial. "Everything is permissible for me" but I will not be mastered by anything. "Food for the stomach and the stomach for food"—but God will destroy them both. The body is not meant for sexual immorality, but for the Lord, and the Lord for the body. By his power God raised the Lord from the dead, and he will raise us also. Do you not know that your bodies are members of Christ himself? . . . Flee from sexual immorality. All other sins a man commits are outside his body, but he who sins sexually sins against his own body. Do you not know that your body is a temple of the Holy Spirit, who is in you, whom you have received from God? You are not your own; you were bought at a price. Therefore honor God with your body."

1 CORINTHIANS 6:12–20 (NIV)

36

WHAT GOD SAYS ABOUT MY BODY

- **My body is God's _____ .**

  You created every part of me; you put me together in my mother's womb . . . I am fearfully and wonderfully made.

  PSALM 139:13–14 (TEV/NIV)

- **God expects me to _____ my body.**

  I will not be mastered by anything.

  1 CORINTHIANS 6:12 (NIV)

- **My body will be _____ after I die.**

  By his power God raised the Lord from the dead, and he will raise us also.

  1 CORINTHIANS 6:14 (NIV)

- **My body is connected to the _____ .**

  Do you not know that your bodies are members of Christ himself?

  1 CORINTHIANS 6:15 (NIV)

Jesus gave his body for you and he wants you to honor him with yours.

- **The Holy Spirit _____ my body.**

  Do you not know that your body is a temple of the Holy Spirit, who is in you, whom you have received from God?

  1 CORINTHIANS 6:19 (NIV)

  Don't you know that you yourselves are God's temple and that God's Spirit lives in you? . . . God's temple is sacred, and you are that temple.

  1 CORINTHIANS 3:16–17 (NIV)

  You are God's dwelling place on earth.

  For we are the temple of the living God.

  2 CORINTHIANS 6:16 (NIV)

- **Jesus _____ on the cross.**

  You are not your own; you were bought at a price. Therefore honor God with your body.

  1 CORINTHIANS 6:19–20 (NIV)

  I urge you, brothers, in view of God's mercy, to offer your bodies as living sacrifices, holy and pleasing to God. This is your spiritual act of worship.

  ROMANS 12:1 (NIV)

  "Do you want to get well?"

  JOHN 5:6 (NIV)

  God wants you to be physically healthy so that you can accomplish great things for his kingdom.

◇ DISCOVERY QUESTIONS
(PICK AT LEAST ONE OR TWO)

- The Bible says **your body is God's property** and that you are the dwelling place of the Holy Spirit. How does that affect the way you see yourself? What do you think you will do differently knowing this fact?

- God expects you to **manage your body**. Why is that so important to God?

- What does it look like to **manage your body**? How good a manager do you think you are?

- Why do you think most Christians tend to put more emphasis on their spirit or mind as opposed to taking care of their bodies?

◈ PUTTING IT INTO PRACTICE

Where do you want to be three months from now with your physical health? What is one thing you will do to take a step in that direction? Not one thing you **could** do, or **might** do, but one thing you **will** do. We know that goals that are not expressed are very rarely met, so share your goal with one other person in your group.

Write your physical health goal in the space below.

MY THREE-MONTH PHYSICAL HEALTH **GOAL**

Now transfer your **Three-Month Physical Health Goal** to your **My Three-Month Goals** list on pages vi to vii.

◈ PRAYER DIRECTION

Spend some time praying for the prayer requests you have been sharing with one another. (Remember to record them on the **Small Group Prayer and Praise Report** on page 218.) You may want to focus on some of the physical challenges or goals you have set in your study this week.

◈ DIVING DEEPER
WANT TO GO DEEPER IN YOUR PHYSICAL HEALTH?

FOR YOU

- Read the **daily devotions** for days 8 to 14 in your workbook.

- Read the **Memory Verse** on page 35 every day this week as part of your quiet time. See if you can have it memorized before your next group meeting.

- Read *The Daniel Plan: 40 Days to a Healthier Life* by Rick Warren, Dr. Daniel Amen, and Dr. Mark Hyman. Not only will you learn how to maximize your **physical health** through **Food** and **Fitness**; you will also be guided through the essentials that bring abundant **health to your Faith**—your relationship with God; **your Focus**—how you think; and **your Friendships**—nurturing healthy relationships with the people you love. Available at **www.saddlebackresources.com**.

- Visit **www.DanielPlan.com** for books and other resources to help you get physically healthy.

FOR THE GROUP

Consider for your next group study **The Daniel Plan** six-week, video-based small group study. It will introduce you to the five essentials for better health: Faith, Food, Fitness, Focus, and Friends. Available at **www.saddlebackresources.com**.

41

THE DANIEL PLAN BOOK

40 Days to a Healthier Life by Rick Warren, Dr. Daniel Amen, and Dr. Mark Hyman is an innovative approach to achieving a healthy lifestyle

THE DANIEL PLAN STARTER PACK (1 DVD AND 1 STUDY GUIDE BUNDLE)

Six sessions on achieving a healthy lifestyle within the key areas of faith, food, fitness, focus, and friends

42

TRANSFORMED IN MY PHYSICAL HEALTH
DAY 8

> *Do you not know that your body is a temple of the Holy Spirit, who is in you, whom you have received from God? You are not your own; you were bought at a price. Therefore honor God with your body.*

1 CORINTHIANS 6:19–20 (NIV)

Our culture tells us that your body belongs to you. It is your property to be used however you see fit, as long as you don't hurt anyone else. As a result, our bodies become idols of worship, and we use them to meet our own felt needs for pleasure, happiness or success. Thus, our culture tells us that our bodies are for the purpose of self-worship.

The Bible radically confronts this kind of thinking about your body. According to God, your body is not your own. It belongs to God. *"You were bought at a price."* He created your body and he has redeemed your body. He paid a high price for your body by sending his only Son to the cross. Jesus had a bodily death and a bodily resurrection so that you might have bodily redemption.

The fact that your body belongs to God has profound implications. As followers of Christ, we reject our cultural belief that our bodies are for self-worship. However, this doesn't mean that we ignore the importance of caring for our bodies. We may not be owners of our bodies, but we are certainly stewards of our bodies. We steward our bodies because they are temples designed to worship God. This means that the primary function of your body is worship. Paul further develops this temple imagery in Romans 12:1 (NIV) when he says, *"Therefore, I urge you, brothers and sisters, in view of God's mercy, to offer your bodies as living sacrifices, holy and pleasing to God—this is your spiritual act of worship."* We are called to offer our bodies to their Owner for his glory and his purpose.

What did you hear?

What do you think?

What will you do?

Now talk to God . . .

> *But he said to me, "My grace is sufficient for you, for my*
> *power is made perfect in weakness."*

We all have weaknesses. Paul uses a great metaphor to remind us how fragile we are, "[We] *have this treasure* [of the gospel] *in jars of clay*" (2 Corinthians 4:7 NIV). Like clay jars, we crack under pressure, experience brokenness, and sometimes fail completely. Unbelievably, there are benefits to weakness.

You know Paul's story. He had a persistent, perplexing problem. He asked God three times to take away his pain. Yet God refused, whispering, *"My grace is all you need, for my power is greatest when you are weak"* (2 Corinthians 12:9 GN).

So, here are **three promises to keep in mind about weaknesses**:

First, **God's power is present in your weakness.** Don't repeatedly resist or resent your limitations. Paul became the church's greatest scholar and missionary while experiencing his challenges.

Second, **God works through weakness to accomplish his task.** Let physical, emotional, psychological and spiritual weaknesses become part of God's providential plan for your life. Some speculate that Paul's letters may never have been written if he was not doubly limited, both physically challenged and incarcerated.

And finally, **God allows limitations to become blessings in disguise.** Paul goes on to say, *"For when I am weak, then I am strong—the less I have, the more I depend upon him"* (2 Corinthians 12:10 LBT). Paul might never have become a great communicator of the gospel if he had been distracted by other things. **His physical pain made him fully dependent on God.**

46

Your limitations are opportunities to trust God's promises more and to have a greater dependence on him. **The more insufficient you are, the more sufficient his grace becomes.**

What did you hear?

What do you think?

What will you do?

Now talk to God . . .

47

TRANSFORMED IN MY PHYSICAL HEALTH
DAY 10

He gives strength to the weary and increases the power of the weak. Even youths grow tired and weary, and young men stumble and fall; but those who hope in the Lord will renew their strength. They will soar on wings like eagles; they will run and not grow weary, they will walk and not be faint.

ISAIAH 40:29–31 (NIV)

Have you ever felt like you've had enough? Have you ever had a day where you felt like you just couldn't go on? Maybe you've been physically worn out by sickness or stress and you've had to make yourself get out of bed in the morning. Or, maybe you've found yourself hopelessly addicted to something and you feel like you'll never have the strength to overcome it. It could be that you struggle with depression or anxiety and every day feels like a chore. **Maybe you've felt like giving up.**

48

If that's you, read that verse again. Look at the promise it contains: *"But those who hope in the Lord **will** renew their strength. They **will** soar on wings like eagles; they **will** run and not grow weary, they **will** walk and not be faint."*

Four times the verse tells us that God will do something for us. Not might, or may, or could or probably will, but **will**. This verse is full of promise for us if we put our hope in the Lord. To hope in the Lord means to trust that God has a plan for your future that will work. **When your situation looks hopeless, you need to put your hope in God and his plan.**

If you are worn out today, put your hope in the Lord. Ask him to renew your strength. Ask him to work out his plan for your future—the plan that will work. And as you do, he promises to give you the physical strength to rise above the things that are holding you down.

What did you hear?

What do you think?

What will you do?

Now talk to God . . .

TRANSFORMED IN MY PHYSICAL HEALTH
DAY 11

I can do all things through Christ who strengthens me.

PHILIPPIANS 4:13 (NKJV)

Great people used by God are just ordinary people with an extraordinary amount of determination. They simply don't know how to give up when the going gets tough. Where do they find this kind of inner strength? Their strength comes from a deep rooted belief that, *"I can do all things through Christ."* Their faith propels them past discouragement and fear into the life God wants them to live—a life completely reliant on God's power, not their own.

What does it take to discourage you in your commitment to physical health? Is it when things don't go your way? How about not reaching your goals? Maybe it's not having the strength to see things through to completion? We often get discouraged because we are doing life on our own power. Our strength and energy have limitations. Our emotional and mental resolve can only last so long. Willpower can only take you so far before it runs out. But God's power is limitless; always available when you need it. There's only one little catch: this power is not automatic. It requires an act of faith called surrender.

In order to be infused with God's strength you must first acknowledge your limitations. You must admit to God that you need him. Total surrender means complete dependence on him day by day, moment by moment. Just like a newly born baby is completely dependent on her mother for everything, **God wants you to be completely dependent on him for all your needs**.

Once you have surrendered and admitted your need, you must ask God for his strength and trust him to deliver. God will not give you all the energy you're going to need for an entire year all at once, but he will give you energy for tomorrow when you get there.

When you feel like you're running on empty and ready to throw in the towel, tap into God's power source. Move past discouragement and step out in faith, trusting God to give you all you need for that day.

50

What did you hear?

What do you think?

What will you do?

Now talk to God . . .

TRANSFORMED IN MY PHYSICAL HEALTH
DAY 12

God has not given us a spirit of fear and timidity, but of power, love, and self-discipline.

2 TIMOTHY 1:7 (NLT)

Self-discipline doesn't come from yourself. It comes from God. We all go through moments of doubt, when the things we know are true and believe in seem to leave us with more questions than answers. There are times in our lives when we get afraid. There are times when we look at the future and are filled with worry. Sometimes we look at a sticky situation and we don't know how we are going to get through it.

But there is a way. When you and I feel powerless over our situations, when we feel afraid of what lies ahead, when our "stick-to-it-iveness" no longer sticks, God is able and willing to give us the power we lack. The courage to face a fear head on doesn't come from within, it comes from God above.

52

The ability to keep going when times get hard comes from trusting in God, not in ourselves. The power to keep up a new habit like dieting or exercise, or to break a bad habit or addiction, doesn't come from you and me gutting it out, but from turning to God and asking him for the power to see our convictions through.

If you are going through a tough time today, if you see something in the future that scares you, if there is something on the horizon that is uncertain, **turn to Jesus and ask him for the power to have faith**. Ask him to give you courage. Ask him to give you boldness to face your fears. If you are striving to start a good habit, or break a bad one, ask him for the self-discipline to see it through.

What did you hear?

What do you think?

What will you do?

53

Now talk to God . . .

TRANSFORMED IN MY PHYSICAL HEALTH
DAY 13

Do not be wise in your own eyes; fear the Lord and shun evil. This will bring health to your body and nourishment to your bones.

PROVERBS 3:7–8 (NIV)

The fear of the Lord is a repeated theme throughout the book of Proverbs. We read in Proverbs 9:10 (NIV), *"The fear of the Lord is the beginning of wisdom."* Reverence and respect for God are the beginning of wisdom. If you think that somehow you're going to develop wisdom for life's decisions without the fear of the Lord, you're just fooling yourself.

What does it mean to fear God? To fear God means you love what he loves and hate what he hates. It means you appreciate who he is and you do what he says. To fear God means you ask for his advice and don't just depend on yourself. To fear God is to treat him with reverence, respect, and awe.

The other option is to be *"wise in your own eyes."* This means that rather than depending upon God, revering and respecting him, you rely upon yourself. It means that you think you know best. Ultimately, this is pride. It is the belief that you are God. Proverbs tells us that this kind of thinking is foolishness.

What this means is that all endeavors must begin with a fear of the Lord rather than trusting in your own wits and resources. In all of life's decisions and actions you must start with God. What does this mean practically? If you desire physical health, start with God rather than your own wisdom. Start by trusting in, listening to, and depending upon God for guidance in your pursuit of physical health. Don't begin with your own strategy and resolve. **Begin with God.**

What did you hear?

What do you think?

What will you do?

55

Now talk to God . . .

TRANSFORMED IN MY PHYSICAL HEALTH
DAY 14

> *I am sure of this, that he who began a good work in you will bring it to completion at the day of Jesus Christ.*

PHILIPPIANS 1:6 (ESV)

Don't give up!

I'm pretty sure that most of us have tried to go on a diet from time to time—and have failed horribly! The first day goes pretty well—up until lunch time! Then, you begin to have second thoughts. Your brain starts talking to you and it can make a pretty convincing argument as to why you deserve to quit your diet and "go ahead and eat heartily!"

> *"You've been working pretty hard! You've got to eat to keep your strength up!"*

> *"Look at that beautiful meal! Someone went to a lot of trouble. Don't offend them! Eat up!"*

> *"You deserve this treat! People don't realize just how much you do around here. Live a little!"*

It's easy to give up in life. And it's easy to give ourselves a good reason to quit.

We start off in the Christian life with the best of intentions. We say, "I can do this!" That's the first mistake. The passage above tells me that it is God who needs to be at work in me. So . . . let God work in you!

Next, we throw ourselves into the Christian life with an inhuman fervor. "I can do this if I try hard enough!" Nope, wrong again. Our confidence must come from knowing that it's God who is putting forth all the effort. So . . . put all your trust in him.

Then, we tell ourselves, "I'm going to make it . . . I'm going to make it . . ." Pretty soon, we are right back where we started and wondering what went wrong. Well, we forgot that it's God who will complete your life in such a way that you will stand victoriously before the throne one day. So . . . **give control of your life to God today.**

Whether it's your diet, your family, or breaking a bad habit, don't quit! **God will never give up on you!** If God starts something, he never stops until his work is perfectly complete. And that means you!

What did you hear?

What do you think?

What will you do?

Now talk to God . . .

NOTES

58

NOTES

59

Origami
book

1      2   3   4

SESSION 3

TRANSFORMED IN MY MENTAL HEALTH

SESSION 3

WEEKEND SERMON NOTES

64

SESSION 3
TRANSFORMED IN MY MENTAL HEALTH

◈ CHECKING IN

- Which of the seven physical health verses from your devotional reading this past week was **the most meaningful to you**?

- What role do you think the mind plays in our growth as followers of Christ?

◈ MEMORY VERSE

Do not conform any longer to the pattern of this world, but be transformed by the renewing of your mind. Then you will be able to test and approve what God's will is—his good, pleasing, and perfect will.

ROMANS 12:2 (NIV)

◈ WATCH THE VIDEO LESSON NOW AND FOLLOW ALONG IN YOUR OUTLINE.

$\rightarrow$

◈ TRANSFORMED IN MY MENTAL HEALTH

WHATEVER GETS YOUR MIND GETS YOU.

> *Though we live in the world, we do not wage war as the world does. The weapons we fight with are not the weapons of the world. On the contrary, they have divine power to demolish strongholds. We demolish arguments and every pretension that sets itself up against the knowledge of God, and we take captive every thought to make it obedient to Christ.*

2 CORINTHIANS 10:3–5 (NIV)

TO MAKE THE MOST OF YOUR MIND . . .

- **Don't believe everything you _____ .**

  You and I have an amazing ability to lie to ourselves. We do it all the time.

  > *The heart is deceitful above all things and beyond cure. Who can understand it?*

  JEREMIAH 17:9 (NIV)

  > *Examine yourselves to see whether you are in the faith; test yourselves.*

  2 CORINTHIANS 13:5 (NIV)

- **Guard your mind against _____ .**

A wise person is hungry for truth, while the fool feeds on trash.

PROVERBS 15:14 (NLT)

There are three types of brain food: toxic food, junk food, and healthy food.

I will not set before my eyes anything that is worthless.

PSALM 101:3 (ESV)

- **Never let up on _____ .**

Intelligent people are always ready to learn. Their ears are open for knowledge.

PROVERBS 18:15 (NLT)

Wise people store up knowledge.

PROVERBS 10:14 (NKJV)

There are two ways to store up knowledge: reading and relationships. Your life will be largely influenced by the books you read and the people you meet.

Those who get wisdom do themselves a favor, and those who love learning will succeed.

PROVERBS 19:8 (NCV)

It's wise to learn from experience. It's wiser to learn from the experiences of others— and it's a lot less painful.

- **Renew your mind daily with _____ .**

Change doesn't start in your behavior. It starts in your thoughts.

67

Don't copy the behavior and customs of this world, but let God transform you into a new person by changing the way you think. Then you will learn to know God's will for you, which is good and pleasing and perfect.

ROMANS 12:2 (NLT)

You will keep in perfect peace all who trust in you, all whose thoughts are fixed on you!

ISAIAH 26:3 (NLT)

- **Let God stretch your _____ .**

Now glory be to God, who by his mighty power at work within us is able to do far more than we would ever dare to ask or even dream of—infinitely beyond our highest prayers, desires, thoughts, or hopes. May he be given glory forever.

EPHESIANS 3:20-21 (TLB)

Nothing happens until somebody starts dreaming. God cannot help you reach your goals if you don't have any goals. He cannot fulfill your dreams if you don't have any dreams. He cannot exceed your expectations if you don't have any expectations.

Where there is no vision, the people perish.

PROVERBS 29:18 (KJV)

God wants you to dream big dreams so you can accomplish great things for his glory.

T _____

H _____

I _____

N _____

K _____

◇ DISCOVERY QUESTIONS
(PICK AT LEAST ONE OR TWO)

- Why is it so easy to **lie to ourselves**?

- Rick talked about **toxic food**, **junk food**, and **healthy food** for your brain. What could you do to give your brain a healthier diet?

- What specific **topics** and **habits** do you want to learn about through your reading and relationships?

- The Bible says, *"You will keep in perfect peace all who trust in you, all whose thoughts are fixed on you!"* (Isaiah 26:3 NLT). What helps you to **fix your thoughts on God**?

PUTTING IT INTO PRACTICE

Where do you want to be three months from now with your mental health? What is one thing you will do to take a step in that direction? Not one thing you **could** do, or **might** do, but one thing you **will** do. Review Rick's video outline to help you with ideas. We know that goals that are not expressed are very rarely met, so share your goal with one other person in your group.

Write your mental health goal in the space below.

MY THREE-MONTH MENTAL HEALTH **GOAL**

Now transfer your **Three-Month Mental Health Goal** to your **My Three-Month Goals** list on pages vi to vii.

PRAYER DIRECTION

In your prayer time this week, focus on the prayer requests from the **Small Group Prayer and Praise Report** on page 218. Also pray for the action steps each person wants to take in the area of Mental Health. You may want to have each person pray for the person on their right going around the circle, or pair up in groups of two.

◈ DIVING DEEPER

WANT TO GO DEEPER IN YOUR MENTAL HEALTH?

FOR YOU

- Read the **daily devotions** for days 15 to 21 in your workbook.

- Read the **Memory Verse** on page 65 every day this week as part of your quiet time. See if you can have it memorized before your next group meeting.

- Read *The Faith: What Christians Believe, Why They Believe It and Why It Matters* by Chuck Colson and Harold Fickett. *The Faith* is a thought-provoking, soul-searching, powerful manifesto of the great, historical, central truths of Christianity that have sustained believers through the centuries. Available at **www.saddlebackresources.com**.

FOR THE GROUP

Consider for your next group study *Wide Angle: Framing Your Worldview*. In this video-based small group study, Rick Warren and Chuck Colson examine worldviews as they relate to the most important questions of our day. They explore such key issues as truth, tolerance, terrorism, reconciliation, and the purpose of life. Available at **www.saddlebackresources.com**.

WIDE ANGLE STUDY GUIDE

Along with the DVD, the study guide explores issues such as truth, tolerance, terrorism, reconciliation, and the purpose of life.

WIDE ANGLE DVD

In this small group study, Rick Warren and Chuck Colson examine worldviews as they relate to the most important questions of our day.

TRANSFORMED IN MY MENTAL HEALTH
DAY 15

You will keep him in perfect peace, whose mind is stayed on you, because he trusts in you.

ISAIAH 26:3 (NKJV)

Do you have **perfect peace** today? I know some days my mind has a mind of its own, and it is anything but peaceful. I can't seem to think clearly about anything. I think about things that **could** happen. I fret over the consequences of what **has** happened. My imagination runs wild with all kinds of negative possibilities. And no matter what I do, I can't seem to bring my thoughts under control. I don't have the "perfect peace" of God. Sound familiar?

The Bible gives the reason for this condition. We don't have perfect peace because our minds are not "stayed" on God. The Hebrew word for "mind" in this verse is not referring to the logical, rational, problem solving part of the mind. Instead, it is the word for imagination. It's our imagination that causes us to lose our peace.

74

The only way to fix it is to fix your mind on God. Get hold of your imagination, grab it by the scruff of the neck, and bring it to God. The Bible says, *"Take captive every thought to make it obedient to Christ"* (2 Corinthians 10:5, NIV). Bring your worries to him in prayer, then change the focus of your attention. Think about God. Lean into God, hold onto him, put your trust in him. When you do, he will give you peace of mind. And when you have peace of mind, then the logical, rational, problem solving part of your mind will be able to think clearly.

When you fix your mind on God, God fixes your mind.

What did you hear?

What do you think?

What will you do?

Now talk to God . . .

TRANSFORMED IN MY MENTAL HEALTH
DAY 16

Do not be anxious about anything, but in everything, by prayer and petition, with thanksgiving, present your requests to God. And the peace of God, which transcends all understanding, will guard your hearts and your minds in Christ Jesus.

PHILIPPIANS 4:6–7 (NIV)

God wants you to be totally free from anxiety. He wants you to live without fear. He wants you to experience his peace *"at all times and in every situation"* (2 Thessalonians 3:16 NLT). God knows that fear and anxiety keep us from living out his purposes for our lives. So he lovingly tells us, *"Don't be anxious about anything."* Anything! Sometimes that's easier said than done.

What is the antidote to anxiety? This verse tells us to pray *"with thanksgiving."* So start with a heart of gratitude. Thank God for his faithfulness and that he has never left your side. Thank him for his unchanging love for you, for his forgiveness and grace. Thank him in advance for what he is going to do!

Next, tell God what's troubling you. Most people pray prayers they think God wants to hear. But God tells us to pray about everything, leaving nothing on the table, and giving it all to him. **If it's big enough to worry about, it's big enough to pray about.**

The result of faithfully bringing your requests to God—with thanksgiving—and trusting him with the outcome is that you will experience *"the peace of God which transcends all understanding."* God's peace is so powerful the Bible says it will even "guard your heart and mind" from the anxieties of this world.

When you give your anxieties to God—your worries of the future, the guilt of your past, your hurts, heartbreaks and struggles—God in return will give you his peace, which is more powerful than any anxiety or problem. His peace will stand guard over your heart and mind like an army protecting a city, watching and keeping you safe from the outside forces that would steal away your joy.

What did you hear?

What do you think?

What will you do?

Now talk to God . . .

TRANSFORMED IN MY MENTAL HEALTH
DAY 17

Finally, brothers, whatever is true, whatever is noble, whatever is right, whatever is pure, whatever is lovely, whatever is admirable—if anything is excellent or praiseworthy—think about such things. Whatever you have learned or received or heard from me, or seen in me—put it into practice. And the God of peace will be with you.

PHILIPPIANS 4:8–9 (NIV)

You are what you think about. Proverbs 23:7 NKJV tells us, *"For as a [man] thinks in his heart, so is he."*

You've probably heard the phrase about computer processing, "garbage in, garbage out." The same is true with your mind. Put garbage in—the types of movies you watch, the internet sites you visit, the music you listen to, the magazines you browse, the books you read—and the output of your life will be garbage too.

So how can you keep the "garbage" out of your mind? You can't just empty your mind of bad thoughts. You must deliberately replace them with something else. Vacuums do not exist naturally in the world, they are artificially created. If you create a vacuum, something fills it. For instance, your gas tank is never empty; it's either filled with gas or with air. The gas replaces the air, the air replaces the gas. Something will always fill a void. Our minds will always be filled with something, but we get to choose what fills them. **So what types of thoughts do you fill your mind with?**

Here's God's list: *"Whatever is true, noble, right, pure, lovely, admirable—if anything is excellent or praiseworthy—think about such things."* The end result is God's peace in your heart. The bottom line is that if a thought doesn't pass this test, don't allow it in your mind. That's easier said than done, which is why the end of the verse says, "put it into practice." God gave you a filter that brings peace of mind. **Practice using it every day!**

DAILY DEVOTIONS: DAY 17

What did you hear?

_____
_____
_____
_____
_____
_____

What do you think?

_____
_____
_____
_____
_____
_____

What will you do?

_____
_____
_____
_____
_____
_____

Now talk to God . . .

_____
_____
_____
_____
_____
_____

TRANSFORMED IN MY MENTAL HEALTH
DAY 18

Do not conform any longer to the pattern of this world, but be transformed by the renewing of your mind. Then you will be able to test and approve what God's will is—his good, pleasing and perfect will.

ROMANS 12:2 (NIV)

Real transformation starts in your mind, not your behavior. You cannot change your character simply be changing your actions. Rather, you change your actions by changing your character. And it all begins with changing the way you think. That's why the Bible says: Don't conform to the ways of the world, *"but be transformed by the renewing of your mind."*

What is the difference between conforming and transforming? To conform something is to change its outward appearance by fitting it into a mold. To transform something is to change its nature. Conforming has to do with behavior. Transforming has to do with character. The Bible is telling us to stop trying to fit in with the ways of the world, but instead allow God to transform our character into the character of Christ.

Notice that conforming is something you do to yourself—you consciously try to fit in or become like everyone else. **But transforming is something that God does to you.** It is God's work in your life, renewing your mind by his grace, through his Word.

God doesn't just want to change what you think, he wants to change how you think— your way of thinking. The Bible says, *"Be made new in the attitude of your mind"* (Ephesians 4:23 NIV).

Then, look at the result of the transformed mind. **God promises that you will be able to discover his will for your life.** Not only will you discover his will, but you will find that it is good, pleasing, and perfect—tailor made for you.

What did you hear?

What do you think?

What will you do?

Now talk to God . . .

TRANSFORMED IN MY MENTAL HEALTH
DAY 19

We have the mind of Christ.

1 CORINTHIANS 2:16 (NIV)

What does it mean to have the mind of Christ? How can we possibly learn to think like he does? If you want to know how Jesus thinks, then you have to know what Jesus has already said. That's why it is so important for us to be people of the Word. If you want to think like Christ, then you have to know the Word of Christ.

You've often heard the popular question, "What would Jesus do?" If you truly want to know what Jesus would do in your situation, then you need to know what he has already said about similar situations. What has Jesus already said about ethics, morality, business, relationships, and money? If you know what he has said, you'll have a pretty good idea of how he thinks and what he would do in your situation. The Bible says, *"Jesus Christ is the same yesterday and today and forever"* (Hebrews 13:8 NIV).

82

The mind of Christ is revealed in the Word of Christ by the Spirit of Christ. The Bible makes it clear that it is the Holy Spirit who makes God's Word understandable to us (see 1 Corinthians 2:9–16). The Holy Spirit is the one who teaches us and enables us to think with the mind of Christ. And he does it by *"expressing spiritual truths in spiritual words"* (verse 13).

You already have the mind of Christ because you have the Spirit of Christ—the Holy Spirit—living in you. **The more you get into the Word of Christ, the more the Spirit of Christ will teach you to think with the mind of Christ.**

What did you hear?

_____

_____

_____

_____

_____

What do you think?

_____

_____

_____

_____

_____

What will you do?

_____

_____

_____

_____

_____

Now talk to God . . .

_____

_____

_____

_____

_____

TRANSFORMED IN MY MENTAL HEALTH
DAY 20

If any of you lacks wisdom, he should ask God, who gives generously to all without finding fault, and it will be given to him.

JAMES 1:5 (NIV)

Do you need wisdom today? God has made an amazing offer that you cannot afford to pass up. He says, *"Ask me, and I will give you the wisdom you need."* So ask . . . but be prepared to act on what he tells you. **God doesn't offer his wisdom as an opinion to be considered at your convenience.** God is not a member of your advisory committee. He is your Lord. His wisdom is truth. **You must act on his wisdom if you want him to give you more.**

You must come to God with a predisposition to obey. Don't ask him what he wants you to do and then decide to say yes. Start with yes, and then he will tell you what to do. If you're asking God for wisdom but heaven seems silent, then you need to ask yourself, "Am I living by the wisdom God has already given me? Have I been guilty of selective obedience?" After all, why should God tell you something if you are ignoring what he has already told you?

God gives wisdom graciously, *"without finding fault."* God will not scold you or make you feel stupid for asking. He wants to give you wisdom because he loves you and wants what is best for you. But he wants you to ask in faith. James goes on to say, *"But when you ask, you must believe and not doubt,"* and not be double-minded (verse 6–8). You must ask God for wisdom, believing that he has the wisdom you are looking for. And you must ask with single-minded determination to live by the wisdom he gives you.

What did you hear?

What do you think?

What will you do?

Now talk to God . . .

TRANSFORMED IN MY MENTAL HEALTH
DAY 21

Those who get wisdom do themselves a favor, and those who love learning will succeed.

PROVERBS 19:8 (NCV)

Wisdom is really not that hard to find, but it can be hard to look for. It all comes down to the choices we make about how we spend our time. We can spend our time wisely and get more wisdom, or we can spend our time foolishly and miss opportunities to grow. Sometimes it's a difficult choice.

Here's a practical suggestion: Trade one hour of gaming or television for one hour of reading every day. Expand your mind by expanding your interests. Use your time wisely and you will be rewarded.

God wants to fill your mind with wisdom, but he won't force it upon you. You must seek it out. The Bible says, *"Blessed are those who find wisdom"*—that means you have to look for it—*"those who gain understanding"*—that means you have to work for it and actively pursue it (Proverbs 3:13 NIV).

What I love about wisdom is that, once found, it can never be lost. In fact, the more wisdom you give away, the more it becomes yours.

So do yourself a favor today. Get some wisdom. And if you will do that, the Bible promises you will succeed.

What did you hear?

What do you think?

What will you do?

Now talk to God . . .

NOTES

NOTES

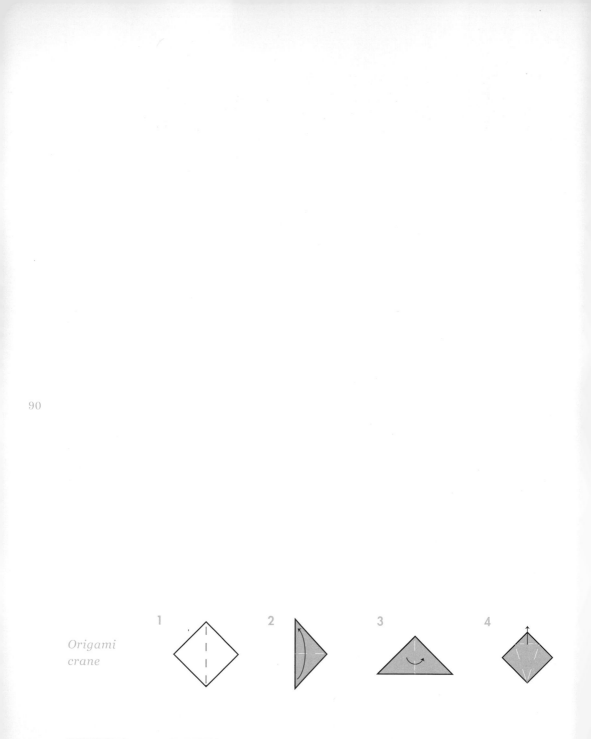

*Origami
crane*

1

2

3

4

TRANSFORMED IN MY EMOTIONAL HEALTH

SESSION 4

WEEKEND SERMON NOTES

93

SESSION 4

SESSION 4
TRANSFORMED IN MY EMOTIONAL HEALTH

◇ CHECKING IN

• Which of the seven mental health verses from your devotional reading this past week was **the most meaningful to you**?

• When you hurt yourself (stub your toe, whack your thumb with a hammer, etc.) do you tend to stuff it, yell at it, cry about it, or dance around?

◇ MEMORY VERSE

"Come to me, all you who are weary and burdened, and I will give you rest."

MATTHEW 11:28 (NIV)

95

◇ WATCH THE VIDEO LESSON NOW AND FOLLOW ALONG IN YOUR OUTLINE.

→

◈ TRANSFORMED IN MY EMOTIONAL HEALTH

He heals the broken-hearted and bandages their wounds.

PSALM 147:3 (TEV)

FIVE STEPS TOWARD EMOTIONAL HEALTH

- _____ my _____ .

You'll never be emotionally healthy until you face your feelings straight on.

> *I kept very quiet . . . but I became even more upset. I became very angry inside, and as I thought about it, my anger burned.*

PSALM 39:2–3 (NCV)

Holding on to hurts is like carrying hot coals in your heart—you're the one who's going to get burned. When you swallow your hurt, your stomach keeps score.

You must be honest with yourself, honest with God, and honest with one other person.

> *When I kept things to myself, I felt weak deep inside me. I moaned all day long.*

PSALM 32:3 (NCV)

- _____ those who have _____ .

One of the most difficult decisions you'll make in life is this: "Do I want to get well or do I want to get even?"

It was while we were still sinners that Christ died for us!

ROMANS 5:8 (TEV)

Get rid of all bitterness, rage and anger, brawling and slander, along with every form of malice. Be kind and compassionate to one another, forgiving each other, just as in Christ God forgave you.

EPHESIANS 4:31–32 (NIV)

You have kept a record of my tears.

PSALM 56:8 (TEV)

Never pay back evil for evil . . . never avenge yourselves. Leave that to God, for he has said that he will repay those who deserve it. [Don't take the law into your own hands.]

ROMANS 12:17–19 (TLB)

- **Replace** _____ **with** _____ .

Let God transform you into a new person by changing the way you think.

ROMANS 12:2 (NLT)

Jesus, who makes people holy, and all those who are made holy have the same Father. That is why Jesus isn't ashamed to call them brothers and sisters.

HEBREWS 2:11 (GWT)

If you want to change the way you feel about your life, you have to change the way you think about your life. Replace old lies with God's truths.

• _____ on the _____ .

> *Put your heart right . . . Reach out to God . . . face the world again, firm and courageous. Then all your troubles will fade from your memory, like floods that are past and remembered no more.*

JOB 11:13-16 (TEV)

Your past is not your future. The old you is not the new you.

> *Look straight ahead with honest confidence; don't hang your head in shame.*

PROVERBS 4:25 (TEV)

• _____ to help _____ .

God wants to redeem your pain. He wants to use your experiences to help other people. That's what ministry is all about.

> [God] *comforts us every time we have trouble, so when others have trouble, we can comfort them with the same comfort God gives us.*

2 CORINTHIANS 1:4 (NCV)

> *When someone becomes a Christian, he becomes a brand new person inside. He is not the same anymore. A new life has begun!*

2 CORINTHIANS 5:17 (TLB)

DISCOVERY QUESTIONS
(PICK AT LEAST ONE OR TWO)

- **God never wastes a hurt.** Your greatest ministry will come from your deepest pain. Would anyone like to share a personal story of how God brought emotional healing into your life? This is great practice for sharing your faith with a non-believing friend.

- The Bible says, *"When I kept things to myself, I felt weak deep inside me. I moaned all day long"* (Psalm 32:3 NCV). Why do you think we would rather hide the things that have happened to us instead of revealing them to someone?

99

- Why is it so hard to forgive when we have been wronged? What happens if we choose not to forgive? What could happen if we do forgive?

- The Bible says, *"Be made new in the attitude of your minds"* (Ephesians 4:23 NIV). Pastor Rick said, "If you want to change the way you feel about your life, you have to change the way you think about your life." What is one thought you need to change about yourself?

◈ PUTTING IT INTO PRACTICE

Where do you want to be three months from now with your emotional health? What is one thing you will do to take a step in that direction? Not one thing you **could** do, or **might** do, but one thing you **will** do. Review Pastor Rick's video outline to help you with ideas. We know that goals that are not expressed are very rarely met, so share your goal with one other person in your group.

Write your emotional health goal in the space below.

MY THREE-MONTH EMOTIONAL HEALTH **GOAL**

Now transfer your **Three-Month Emotional Health Goal** to your **My Three-Month Goals** list on pages vi to vii.

◈ PRAYER DIRECTION

Spend some time praying for one another's requests from the **Small Groups Prayer and Praise Report** on page 218. If anyone shared a hurt or needs prayer, be sure to pray for those things during your prayer time. If you are short on time or your group members would feel more comfortable sharing with one other person, you might want to pair up and pray for each other.

◈ DIVING DEEPER
WANT TO GO DEEPER IN YOUR EMOTIONAL HEALTH?

FOR YOU

- Read the **daily devotions** for days 22 to 28 in your workbook.

- Read the **Memory Verse** on page 95 every day this week as part of your quiet time. See if you can have it memorized before your next group meeting.

- Read *Life's Healing Choices* by John Baker. Based on the eight beatitudes of Jesus, *Life's Healing Choices* offers freedom from our hurts, hang-ups, and habits through eight healing choices that promise true happiness and life transformation. Available at **www.saddlebackresources.com**.

FOR THE GROUP

Consider for your next group study *Life's Healing Choices Small Group Study*. This eight-week video-based small group study looks at each of the Beatitudes from Jesus' Sermon on the Mount and takes you step-by-step through the recovery and self-discovery process. Available at **www.saddlebackresources.com**.

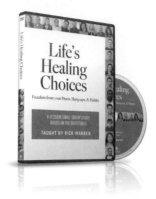

LIFE'S HEALING CHOICES BOOK

Life's Healing Choices offers
freedom from our hurts, hang-ups,
and habits through eight healing
choices that promise true happiness
and life transformation.

LIFE'S HEALING CHOICES DVD

This 8-session DVD takes you
through each of the Beatitudes from
Jesus' Sermon on the Mount.

SADDLEBACKRESOURCES.COM

> *"Come to me, all you who are weary and burdened, and I will give you rest. Take my yoke upon you and learn from me, for I am gentle and humble in heart, and you will find rest for your souls. For my yoke is easy and my burden is light."*

MATTHEW 11:28–30 (NIV)

In the Bible, people came to Jesus for many reasons. Some came to be healed. Others needed advice. Many came for eternal life. Jesus gives you another reason to come to him: rest from your burdens. But here's the catch. Once you have come to Jesus with your burdens, you have to give up control. Jesus says, *"Take my yoke upon you."*

A yoke is a farming tool. Farmers yoke their plow-horses together to keep them going in the same direction and at the same pace. When they are yoked together, one cannot go faster than the other, or slower for that matter. They are less prone to veer off the path when they are working together. When their burden is cut in half, they can accomplish twice as much.

Jesus is using a yoke as a symbol of partnership with him. God never intended for you to bear your burdens alone. **Jesus is saying, "I will help carry the load, you don't have to do it alone anymore. When you're weary and worn out, emotionally exhausted, let me carry your burden with you."**

Jesus' invitation is, *"Learn from me, for I am gentle and humble in heart, and you will find rest for your souls."* The secret to overcoming an overloaded life is to go to the only One who can truly give you rest for your soul. Jesus is your burden bearer, your model for stress-free living. Accept his invitation today and find the rest you have been searching for.

104

What did you hear?

What do you think?

What will you do?

Now talk to God . . .

> *"Peace I leave with you; my peace I give you. I do not give to you as the world gives. Do not let your hearts be troubled and do not be afraid."*

JOHN 14:27 (NIV)

Someone has calculated that there have been 286 years of peace in the last 3,500 years of human history. That's a horrible track record. The peace of the world is fleeting and fragile.

Where conflict reigns, fear also rules. Fear and hatred are profound influences on you and me. Scientists speculate that prolonged fear, hatred, conflict, and unforgiveness actually alter our DNA. When peace is missing, we are fragmented and flawed.

God's promise is forever-peace. In his last days on earth, Jesus comforted his anxious disciples: *"I leave with you peace. I give you my own peace, and my gift is nothing like the peace of this world. You must not be distressed and you must not be daunted,"* (PH). The Master knew that his disciples were anxiously grappling with twin realities: touching and talking to him was ending, and his death seemed imminent. Jesus provided forever-peace to return emotional stability to his faltering disciples.

But just what is forever-peace? According to Script

- God's peace is a gift. You don't work for it, earn it, psyche yourself up for it, or try really hard to get it. You just accept it.

- God's peace does not depend on circumstances. His peace is present in terrible, terrifying, tortuous times. Know why?

- God's peace, *shalom* in Jesus' language, means more than the absence of conflict, it's the presence of all things good!

106

The bottom line is that God's promise of forever-peace is fulfilled by his forever-presence! So *"do not let your hearts be troubled and do not be afraid."* Don't focus on the absence of peace; focus on the presence of God, and his peace will come to you.

What did you hear?

What do you think?

What will you do?

Now talk to God . . .

107

TRANSFORMED IN MY EMOTIONAL HEALTH
DAY 24

The Lord is my Shepherd . . . Even though I walk through the valley of the shadow of death, I will fear no evil, for you are with me; your rod and your staff, they comfort me.

PSALM 23:1,4 (NIV)

God will always be with you. You will never have to go through life alone. You won't have any experience that God does not see. He is walking right beside you, even when you walk *"through the valley of the shadow of death."* The difference for those who follow Christ is not the absence of the shadow of death, but the presence of the Shepherd. In fact, because of the Shepherd, death is now just a shadow of its former self. Not even death can separate you from God's love. In every situation, God is there.

When the Shepherd walks with you he carries a rod, just in case you need a little prodding to keep moving. The purpose for the rod is not to hurt the sheep, but to lead the sheep. Sometimes we need a good poke! God uses his rod to let you know, "You can do it! Don't quit! Don't stop or give up! I am right here with you!"

The Shepherd also carries his staff as he walks with you. He uses his staff to protect you from your enemy. Your Shepherd can easily deal with any threat by his mighty power. So you do not have to fear evil.

You are not alone. God is with you. He'll get you through life. And he'll get you through death. He'll bring you home safely. And you will dwell in the house of the Lord, forever.

What did you hear?

What do you think?

What will you do?

Now talk to God . . .

TRANSFORMED IN MY EMOTIONAL HEALTH
DAY 25

The eternal God is your refuge, and underneath are the everlasting arms.

DEUTERONOMY 33:27 (NIV)

Most of us like a hug when we are feeling down. The problem is, there's not always someone there to give us one when we want it. We know this for sure, there will be tough times. There will be circumstances beyond your control, and crises that come out of nowhere. The pain will seem greater than you can bear. It's then, when things look impossible, that you must remember to run to your Heavenly Father. He will be there. He is always there.

God sees your pain. He hears your cry. He counts every tear you shed. He stands ready to help. You just need to come to him. He is your shelter in the storm. His everlasting arms are strong and waiting to embrace you. In them you will find peace, protection, and strength. And when you allow him to hold you close, to wrap his arms around you, he will be with you until the storm passes and joy comes in the morning.

It's hard to imagine that the God who created the universe wants to be there for you, but he does. **His greatest desire is to draw you close to him.** This is why he created you. So when you're feeling like no one cares, and your thoughts lead you into a pit of despair, call on the Lord to pull you out. His lovingkindness never fails. He wants nothing more than to give you that hug you need.

What did you hear?

_____

_____

_____

_____

_____

What do you think?

_____

_____

_____

_____

_____

What will you do?

_____

_____

_____

_____

_____

Now talk to God . . .

_____

_____

_____

_____

_____

> *Therefore, there is now no condemnation for those who are in Christ Jesus.*

Imagine that I asked you to write down all of the bad things you have ever done on a 3×5 card. Don't worry, I'm not going to ask you to do that. Besides, if you're at all like me, a 3×5 card wouldn't be nearly enough room for all of that stuff! But just imagine that I did. Now, picture putting that card with every sin, every careless word, every stupid mistake, everything you feel guilty about, inside of a hardback book. Now, close the book.

Can you still see the card? No. It's still there, but you can't see it. It's inside something bigger, something better. That card is still there, but it is **in** something else. That's what it's like to be in Christ Jesus. It means that once we put our faith in Christ, once we ask him to forgive us for our sins, God simply doesn't see them anymore. We are declared not guilty. Not because we didn't do the things on that card, but because he chooses to see Jesus instead of our mistakes.

You may be carrying something around that you feel terribly guilty about. You may feel like this guilt comes from God to remind you, or punish you, for what you have done. But that is simply not the case. Jesus forgives us of our sins and takes them from us. When Jesus went to the cross he paid the price for your sins, once and for all. You don't have to keep paying for your sins through guilt. You don't have to carry them around anymore. You don't have to live with shame anymore.

If you are in Christ, you are forgiven.

What did you hear?

_____
_____
_____
_____

What do you think?

_____
_____
_____
_____

What will you do?

_____
_____
_____
_____

Now talk to God . . .

_____
_____
_____
_____

TRANSFORMED IN MY EMOTIONAL HEALTH
DAY 27

The joy of the Lord is your strength.

NEHEMIAH 8:10 (NIV)

The secret to strength is joy. It's not your desire or your determination that are your strength. It's your joy. This means that one of the main reasons you feel you can't do something or don't have the strength to face something is a lack of joy. When you have joy, then you are able to find security in the truth that God has a plan, and you have strength for that day.

Joy gives you strength for life's greatest challenges. Mother Teresa's job description for working with the sick from the streets of Calcutta was two simple items: desire to work hard and have a joyful attitude. When you work hard but have no joy, you'll find yourself feeling worn down by life, emotionally, physically, and spiritually exhausted.

114

How do you experience joy? The Westminster Catechism states, "The chief end of man is to glorify God and to enjoy him forever." Eternity is going to be filled with the sound of human laugher, people enjoying God. You don't have to wait to get in on that party, you can choose today to enjoy the goodness and greatness of God.

Nehemiah tells us that it's the *"joy of the Lord"* that we are choosing. Joy is not a matter of trying to work up good feelings about yourself or the world around you. Sometimes there's little to feel good about there. True joy centers on God. The joy that God gives starts by focusing on who God is.

Whatever circumstances you are facing right now, spend a few moments thinking about who God is. **Think about his grace, power, forgiveness, and patience. Think about his comfort and love.** Let the joy that flows from remembering who God is become your strength for what you are facing today.

What did you hear?

What do you think?

What will you do?

Now talk to God . . .

TRANSFORMED IN MY EMOTIONAL HEALTH
DAY 28

He who dwells in the shelter of the Most High will rest in the shadow of the Almighty. I will say of the Lord, "He is my refuge and my fortress, my God, in whom I trust."

PSALM 91:1–2 (NIV)

I love New York City. It is a huge and important world center where the nations come to meet and exchange ideas and share their cultures. And what a humbling place it is! You are surrounded by monolithic buildings that are at once both beautifully iconic and gigantic in stature. As you walk through the streets of downtown, even in the daytime, you are engulfed by the shadows of these gargantuan skyscrapers that blot out the sun. The city is enormous in every way.

God is just like that city.

The scripture above says that you can dwell in him. He is a whole life for you. You find food and sustenance and love and beauty and truth in him. He is a city unto himself. **Dwell in him.**

He shelters you. He can protect you from whatever life throws at you. He is so big and absolutely sovereign that nothing can touch you except what he allows. And he only allows exactly what is right for you. **Hide in him.**

He is so big that you can't go anywhere that he is not in control. His shadow is so vast that it falls on everything, everywhere, and everyone on the earth. No matter where you find yourself in this world and no matter what condition you are in, you can always rest in his shadow and find the help you need. **Rest in him.**

God is unbeatably strong, preeminently vast, and unstoppably powerful. He truly is a fortress and our refuge. **Trust in him.**

If life is getting you down, go to the City of the King and take refuge in his greatness, rest in his shadow, and rely upon him to see you through. **He will never fail you.**

What did you hear?

_____

_____

_____

_____

What do you think?

_____

_____

_____

_____

_____

What will you do?

_____

_____

_____

_____

_____

Now talk to God . . .

_____

_____

_____

_____

_____

NOTES

NOTES

119

*Origami
heart*

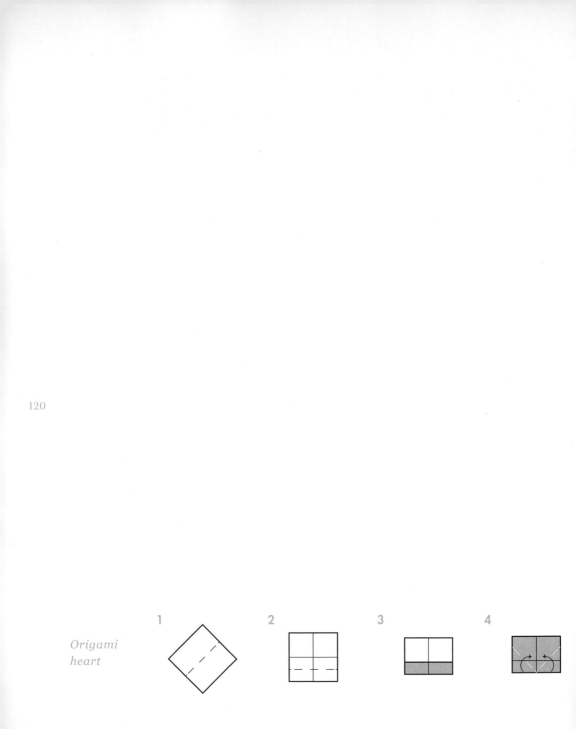

1 2 3 4

TRANSFORMED
IN MY
RELATIONAL
HEALTH

SESSION 5

6   7   8   9

WEEKEND SERMON NOTES

SESSION 5

TRANSFORMED IN MY RELATIONAL HEALTH

◇ CHECKING IN

- Which of the seven emotional health verses from your devotional reading this past week was **the most meaningful to you**?

- When it comes to personal conflict, are you a skunk or a turtle? Turtles withdraw quietly into their shells until the trouble is past. When skunks are in conflict, they let everybody know about it.

◈ MEMORY VERSE

125

Above all, love each other deeply, because love covers over a multitude of sins.

1 PETER 4:8 (NIV)

◈ WATCH THE VIDEO LESSON NOW AND FOLLOW ALONG IN YOUR OUTLINE.

→

◈ TRANSFORMED IN MY RELATIONAL HEALTH

TWO KINDS OF FRIENDS

- _____ friends are the result of _____ .

- _____ friends are the result of _____ .

> _A mirror reflects a man's face, but what he is really like is shown by the kind of friends he chooses._
>
> PROVERBS 27:19 (TLB)

> _The righteous choose their friends carefully._
>
> PROVERBS 12:26 (NIV)

FIVE KINDS OF PEOPLE TO AVOID AS CLOSE FRIENDS

- _____ people

> _Our friends, we command you in the name of our Lord Jesus Christ to keep away from all believers who are living a lazy life . . ._
>
> 2 THESSALONIANS 3:6 (TEV)

- _____ people

> _Don't make friends with people who have hot, violent tempers. You might learn their habits and not be able to change._
>
> PROVERBS 22:24–25 (TEV)

* _____ **people**

> *I told you not to associate with immoral people. Now I did not mean [unbelievers] who are immoral or greedy or are thieves, or who worship idols. To avoid them you would have to get out of the world completely. What I meant was that you should not associate with a person who calls himself a believer but is immoral or greedy or worships idols or is a slanderer or a drunkard or a thief. Don't even sit down to eat with such a person.*

1 CORINTHIANS 5:9–11 (TEV)

* _____ **people**

> *Do not eat the food of a stingy man . . . for he is the kind of man who is always thinking about the cost. 'Eat and drink,' he says to you, but his heart is not with you.*

PROVERBS 23:6–7 (NIV)

* _____ **people**

> *Don't team up with those who are unbelievers.*

2 CORINTHIANS 6:14a (NLT)

CHOOSE CLOSE FRIENDS WHO WILL . . .

* _____ **me mentally**

> *He who walks with the wise grows wise.*

PROVERBS 13:20a (NIV)

As iron sharpens iron, so one man sharpens another.

PROVERBS 27:17 (NIV)

• _____ **me emotionally**

A friend loves at all times, and a brother is born for adversity.

PROVERBS 17:17 (NIV)

Bear one another's burdens.

GALATIANS 6:2 (NKJV)

• _____ **me spiritually**

Encourage one another and build each other up.

1 THESSALONIANS 5:11 (NIV)

Spur one another on toward love and good deeds.

HEBREWS 10:24 (NIV)

How can I attract that kind of friend? By being that kind of friend.

HOW TO BUILD HEALTHY FRIENDSHIPS

• **Get interested in** _____ .

Unfriendly people care only about themselves.

PROVERBS 18:1 (NLT)

Let each of you look out not only for his own interests, but also for the interests of others.

PHILIPPIANS 2:4 (NKJV)

- **Don't be a** _____ .

   Do everything without complaining and arguing, so that no one can criticize you. Live clean, innocent lives as children of God, shining like bright lights in a world full of crooked and perverse people.

PHILIPPIANS 2:14-15 (NLT)

- **Be a** _____ .

   Be quick to listen and slow to speak.

JAMES 1:19 (CEV)

   Counsel in the heart of man is like deep water; but a man of understanding will draw it out.

PROVERBS 20:5 (KJV)

129

- **Accept people** _____ .

   Accept one another . . . just as Christ accepted you.

ROMANS 15:7 (NIV)

   A friend loves at all times.

PROVERBS 17:17A (NIV)

- **Help people** _____ .

   Honor one another above yourselves.

ROMANS 12:10 (NIV)

Don't be selfish; don't try to impress others. Be humble, thinking of others as better than yourselves.

PHILIPPIANS 2:3 (NLT)

- **Be** _____ .

Rejoice with those who rejoice, and weep with those who weep.

ROMANS 12:15 (NKJV)

- **Stick with them in** _____ .

There are "friends" who pretend to be friends, but there is a friend who sticks closer than a brother.

PROVERBS 18:24 (TLB)

Two are better than one because . . . if one falls down, his friend can help him up. But pity the man who falls and has no one to help him up!

ECCLESIASTES 4:9–10 (NIV)

130

- **Share** _____ **with them.**

"Go back home and tell everyone how much God has done for you." The man then went all over town, telling everything that Jesus had done for him.

LUKE 8:39 (CEV)

"Do to others as you would have them do to you."

LUKE 6:31 (NIV)

"I do not call you servants any longer . . . Instead, I call you friends."

JOHN 15:15 (TEV)

◇ DISCOVERY QUESTIONS
(PICK AT LEAST ONE OR TWO)

- The Bible says, *"Spur one another on toward love and good deeds."* (Hebrews 10:24 NIV) We all need spiritual encouragers in our lives. Who is a spiritual encourager to you? What are some ways they encourage you?

- Review the three qualities of a close friend: People who challenge you mentally, support you emotionally, and strengthen you spiritually. Remember, to find that kind of friend, you need to be that kind of friend. Which of these characteristics do you need to develop in your own life?

132

- Which of Pastor Rick's eight ways to build healthy friendships is the most important to you and why?

PUTTING IT INTO PRACTICE

Where do you want to be three months from now with your relational health? What is one thing you will do to take a step in that direction? Not one thing you **could** do, or **might** do, but one thing you **will** do. Review Rick's video outline to help you with ideas. We know that goals that are not expressed are very rarely met, so share your goal with one other person in your group.

Write your relational health goal in the space below.

MY THREE-MONTH RELATIONAL HEALTH **GOAL**
_____

Now transfer your **Three-Month Relational Health Goal** to your **My Three-Month Goals** list on pages vi to vii.

PRAYER DIRECTION

- Do you have any friends who don't know Jesus Christ? Pray for their salvation with your group.

- Be sure to pray for the requests in the **Small Group Prayer and Praise List** on page 218.

- Pray together about your three-month goal to build healthy relationships.

◈ DIVING DEEPER
WANT TO GO DEEPER IN YOUR RELATIONAL HEALTH?

FOR YOU

- Read the **daily devotions** for days 29 to 35 in your workbook.

- Read the **Memory Verse** on page 125 every day this week as part of your quiet time. See if you can have it memorized before your next group meeting.

- Read *The Relationship Principles of Jesus* by Tom Holladay. Based on an exhaustive study of what Jesus did and said about relationships, this book guides readers on a forty-day journey that will bring new health and richness to their marriages, families, friendships, and all the relationships in their lives. Available at **www.saddlebackresources.com**.

FOR THE GROUP

Consider for your next group study *40 Days of Love*. In this video-based small group study, Rick Warren teaches biblical principles for healthy, loving relationships. The more we learn how to love authentically, the more we become like Jesus. Available at **www.saddlebackresources.com**.

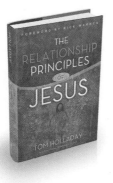

THE RELATIONSHIP PRINCIPLES OF JESUS

In forty days, bring new depth and health to your marriage, your family, and your friendships. Six weeks to explore and implement six foundational principles that Jesus taught and lived.

40 DAYS OF LOVE DVD

Used with the *40 Days of Love* Study Guide, this 6-session study will bring new depth and health to your marriage.

SADDLEBACKRESOURCES.COM

"I am the vine; you are the branches. If you remain in me and I in you, you will bear much fruit; apart from me you can do nothing."

JOHN 15:5 (NIV)

Jesus' invitation to remain in him is at the very heart of his gospel. **As a branch depends upon a vine to bear fruit, so likewise we must depend upon Jesus to bear fruit in our lives.**

It is only by abiding in relational intimacy with Jesus that we can hope to bear the fruit of the Spirit in our relationships with others.

Jesus emphatically makes this point when he says, *"If you remain in me and I in you, you will bear **much** fruit; apart from me you can do **nothing**."* Notice the strong language. If we abide in loving relationship with him we will produce "a little fruit"? No, we will produce "much fruit." We will flourish. On the other hand, if we do not abide in him we can still do a "something"? No, we can do "nothing." In fact, in the Greek this sentence is a double negative and so it really can be read, "you can do nothing, really nothing." Jesus wants to make sure we get his point loud and clear.

The only way to bear fruit is to abide in relationship with Jesus. If we want to be the kind of people who love, who are patient, who are kind, who are gentle, who are self-controlled, (Galatians 5:22–23) we must remain in him. Bearing fruit is not a result of our resolve or determination. It is the result of abiding in a dependent relationship with Jesus by the Holy Spirit. The fruit of the Spirit is just that, the fruit of **the Spirit**. It is a result of God's transforming power, not our willpower. It is produced by the Holy Spirit who now makes our heart his home.

What did you hear?

_____
_____
_____
_____
_____

What do you think?

_____
_____
_____
_____
_____

What will you do?

_____
_____
_____
_____
_____

Now talk to God . . .

_____
_____
_____
_____
_____

TRANSFORMED IN MY RELATIONAL HEALTH
DAY 30

"Blessed are the merciful, for they will be shown mercy."

MATTHEW 5:7 (NIV)

Thank God for his mercy! In our brokenness and sin we certainly need it. He has shown us mercy at the cross by taking upon himself the very punishment we deserved. The Holy Spirit continues to pour out his life giving, life sustaining mercy in our lives. Like a cascading fountain, *"His mercies never come to an end; they are new every morning"* (Lamentations 3:22–23 ESV).

God calls us to drink deeply of his overflowing mercy. He calls us to return to the fountain day after day that we might become intimately acquainted with his mercy. As those who personally know the mercy of God, we are to be people of mercy ourselves. As those who have been blessed with the mercy of God, we are to bless others with the same grace, patience, and care that we have received from him. We are not called to dole out judgment or give people what they deserve, but instead to be gracious and merciful.

Do you want to be a person of mercy? If you drink deeply from God's fountain of mercy, then the mercy of God will overflow in your life. If you are aware of how much you need God's mercy, your heart will be softened toward others in need of mercy. **Jesus' mercy toward sinners and social outcasts was a radical display of God's love in the culture of his day.** It's just as powerful—and unexpected—in our culture of self-centeredness and judgment today. As we extend mercy, grace, compassion, and forgiveness to the forgotten, the marginalized, and the rejected, we will point people to the mercy of Jesus.

138

What did you hear?

_____
_____
_____
_____
_____

What do you think?

_____
_____
_____
_____
_____

What will you do?

_____
_____
_____
_____
_____

Now talk to God . . .

_____
_____
_____
_____
_____

"Blessed are the peacemakers, for they will be called children of God."

MATTHEW 5:9 (NIV)

What does it mean to be blessed? The word for blessing in Greek is "makarios," which can more literally be translated "happy." So, Jesus tells us, "Happy are the peacemakers." He does not say, "Happy are the peace lovers." Everybody loves peace. Nor does he say, "Happy are the peaceable," those who never get disturbed by anything. Rather, he tells us "happy" are those who make peace—who actively seek to resolve conflict.

What kind of happiness are we talking about here? Does Jesus mean that all the circumstances of our lives will work out the way we want them to? No, that's not the point. Jesus does not mean that we will always "feel" happy based on our current life circumstances, but rather that we are in a position of happiness because we have relationship with God. **To be happy is to be at peace with God.**

God is a peacemaker. In fact, he is The Peacemaker. Through the cross of Jesus Christ, God has made peace with us who warred with him in our sin. We were once enemies of God and now we are called children of God (Colossians 1:21). We must delight in the peace we have with The Peacemaker. It is a peace found deep within our souls, a peace that passes human understanding. To be at peace with God means we have been reconciled to right relationship with him.

God calls us to follow his lead. He calls us to share the very peace we have found in him with the rest of the world. He wants us to be known as peacemakers. He wants us to reflect his redeeming and reconciling love to the world around us. For only his children truly know what real peace, ultimate peace, life giving peace, is all about. In a world of conflict, strife, and revenge we can be a profound witness of The Peacemaker by being peacemakers ourselves.

What did you hear?

What do you think?

What will you do?

Now talk to God . . .

TRANSFORMED IN MY RELATIONAL HEALTH
DAY 32

"But love your enemies, do good to them, and lend to them without expecting to get anything back. Then your reward will be great, and you will be sons of the Most High, because he is kind to the ungrateful and wicked."

LUKE 6:35 (NIV)

Love your enemies. If ever we missed the radical nature of Jesus' message, here it is, loud and clear. **Jesus calls us to love those who do not love us.** To love those who have wounded us. To love those who slander our name or gossip about us. Just a few verses prior to this Jesus says, *"Love your enemies, do good to those who hate you, bless those who curse you, pray for those who mistreat you"* (Luke 6:27–28 NIV). If this isn't radical living, I don't know what is.

We get a clear picture of this radical kind of love in Jesus' life. As he hung upon the cross, wounded, mocked and ridiculed, Jesus cried out, *"Father, forgive them, for they do not know what they are doing"* (Luke 23:34 NIV). **In the midst of his pain and suffering Jesus extended love to his enemies.** He prayed for their forgiveness. Not only does this scene give us a model for loving our enemies, but it reminds us of the profound truth of God's love for us. As Scripture tells us, it was while we were enemies of God ourselves that Christ Jesus died for us so that we could be reconciled to God (Romans 5:10). In a very real sense, Jesus' prayer for forgiveness extends to us, for in our sin we stand with his accusers, persecutors, and mockers.

We know we do not merit God's favor and yet he has freely and fully poured out his love and grace upon us. It is this kind of love that transforms our hearts and makes us more like Jesus, so that we can display his radical love even to our enemies, or perhaps, especially to them.

What did you hear?

What do you think?

What will you do?

Now talk to God . . .

TRANSFORMED IN MY RELATIONAL HEALTH
DAY 33

Above all, love each other deeply, because love covers over a multitude of sins.

1 PETER 4:8 (NIV)

Love is all you need. That's pretty simple isn't it?

The grammar in this passage is very interesting here. Now, don't tune out just because you heard the word "grammar." Listen to this: It is just as acceptable, in the original language, for the verse to be read one of two different ways.

You could say: "When I truly love you in a deep way, I will forgive you completely and tenderly." Or, you could say: "When I love you deeply, God himself will forgive my multitude of sins."

Either way, love is all you need. This means that I have been called upon, by God, to love you in such a way that I quickly drop any offense that I might have toward you. I live a life of love and accept you, warts and all, just as Jesus accepts you—and how he has accepted me too for that matter. It also means that when I learn to love you in this way, God exercises his forgiveness towards me and I live a life that is filled with grace, acceptance, and the favor of God. Love is all you need!

So how do I do it? Here are some ways to love from 1 Corinthians 13:4–8. (Go see for yourself.)

Be patient with someone today who is a little slower than you when it comes to "getting it."
Be kind to someone who needs a little extra help—offer it to them without their having to beg you for it.
Don't boast about yourself today. Find someone else to be proud of and let them know it!
Don't get angry. Stay cool. Take a deep breath and carefully explain your feelings by building a bridge into someone else's life, rather than a wall.

Be protective. Stand up for someone who could use a little extra strength to turn their circumstances around.

Don't give up on anyone. Keep the faith. Hang in there. Renew your hope. Persevere in your love for them.

Love is all you need. So now do it! Love someone else today and you **will** be graciously loved by God.

What did you hear

What do you think?

145.

What will you do?

Now talk to God . . .

TRANSFORMED IN MY RELATIONAL HEALTH
DAY 34

He heals the brokenhearted and binds up their wounds.

Sticks and stones may break your bones . . . but words can break your heart.

Broken bones heal. But it takes time. When my eight year old son broke his arm, we had to go to the doctor and get x-rays. Then the bones were patched up and set in place. Next came the plaster cast to hold everything together. Finally, it was time to go home. For the next few days there was quite a bit of pain, which required his mother and me to show compassion and care as we addressed all of his needs. He lost the full use of his arm for a month or so, but then he was back to playing, pitching a baseball, and climbing trees.

God's process for healing a broken heart is a lot like healing a broken bone.

Pray. Come to God and let him know that you are in pain. He will listen carefully. He will know exactly what to do.

Listen. Give God a chance to look into your heart and life, just like an x-ray, and make his own assessment of what needs to take place. Trust him. He can read your charts much better than you can.

Rest. God will put his arms of love around you and hold everything that is broken together with the plaster of his kindness and strong compassion. He will comfort you with his promises and surround you with his people, the church, who will hold you up while you heal.

Trust. You might find that you are not fully functional for a while. There will be some pain. Share your hurts with others that you can trust—people in the Body that under-stand and will nurse you back to health. But, just like healing a broken bone, you can't do it alone.

DAILY DEVOTIONS: DAY 34

Rejoice. One day, when the healing is done, you will laugh again and face life with hopefulness and joy. You can count on God. You have his word on it. *"He heals the brokenhearted and binds up their wounds."*

What did you hear?

What do you think?

What will you do?

Now talk to God . . .

TRANSFORMED IN MY RELATIONAL HEALTH
DAY 35

Cast all your care upon him, for he cares for you.

1 PETER 5:7 (NKJV)

At first glance, this verse is a promising invitation to de-complicate life. Peter apparently counsels us to "dump and run," casting our problems on God, because he's somehow obliged to relieve us from difficulties. Is Peter advising us to avoid responsibility for our troubles? Or is this reading naïve, especially as it relates to relationships and their inevitable anxieties and conflicts?

In its context, this verse actually encourages Christians to become mature and to embrace their responsibilities. Peter identifies the key to "casting our cares" as humility: *"God gives grace to the humble. Therefore, humble yourselves under the mighty hand of God that he may exalt you in due time, casting all your care upon him, for he cares for you."* (1 Peter 5:5–7, NKJV). Why does Peter connect our cares with humility before God?

148

Humility is seeing ourselves in relationship with God—Father, Son and Holy Spirit—"The I AM," "The ALWAYS." God is described in Scripture as loving, good, wise, gracious, merciful, never-changing, all-powerful, all-knowing, everywhere-at-once, sovereign, before all, over all, in all, through all, and so much more! Humility stands in rapt attention before God and exclaims, "I'm not worthy!" Humility acknowledges and acts on one profound truth, "You are God, and I am NOT!"

And it is this God who says to the humble, "Do you need my grace in a relationship right now? Cast all of your cares on me, because I care for you. Bring me every heartbreak, every disappointment, every conflict. It's all important to me because you're important to me. I care about your relationships. And because you have humbly asked, I will pour out my grace upon your life."

When you are worried about a relationship, do what Peter says: **humble yourself before God, cast your care upon him, and receive his grace.**

What did you hear?

_____
_____
_____
_____
_____

What do you think?

_____
_____
_____
_____
_____
_____
_____

What will you do?

_____
_____
_____
_____
_____
_____

Now talk to God . . .

_____
_____
_____
_____
_____

NOTES

NOTES

151

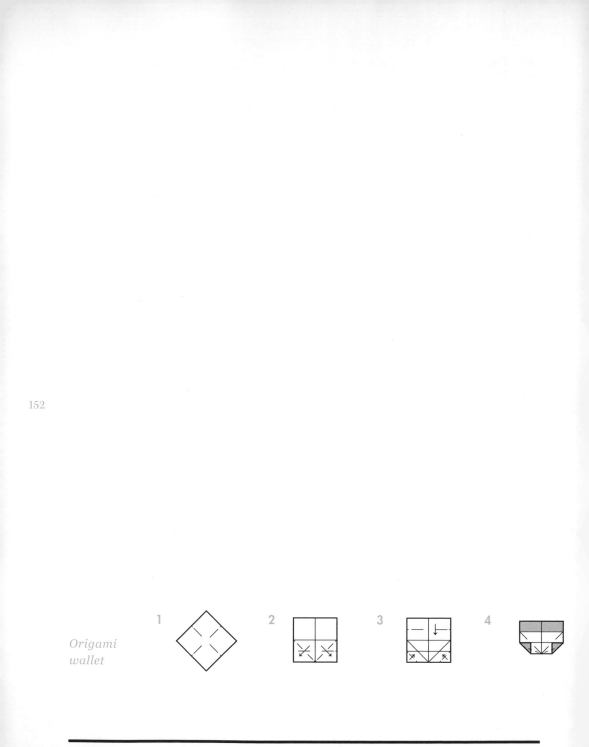

*Origami
wallet*

1   2   3   4

TRANSFORMED IN MY FINANCIAL HEALTH

SESSION 6

WEEKEND SERMON NOTES

SESSION 6

TRANSFORMED IN MY FINANCIAL HEALTH

◇ CHECKING IN

- Which of the seven relational health verses from your devotional reading this past week was **the most meaningful to you**?

- When it comes to money are you more of a **saver or a spender**?

◇ MEMORY VERSE

Honor the Lord with your wealth, with the firstfruits of all your crops; then your barns will be filled to overflowing, and your vats will brim over with new wine.

PROVERBS 3:9–10 (NIV)

157

◇ WATCH THE VIDEO LESSON NOW AND FOLLOW ALONG IN YOUR OUTLINE.

→

◈ TRANSFORMED IN MY FINANCIAL HEALTH

SEVEN HABITS FOR FINANCIAL HEALTH

- **I must trust God as my _____ and _____ .**

  Everything comes from [God] and exists by his power and is intended for his glory.

  ROMANS 11:36 (NLT)

  Remember the Lord your God, for it is he who gives you the ability to produce wealth.

  DEUTERONOMY 8:18 (NIV)

- **I must keep _____.**

  Riches can disappear fast . . . so watch your business interests closely. Know the state of your flocks and your herds.

  PROVERBS 27:23–24 (TLB)

- **I must give the first _____ back to God.**

  The purpose of tithing is to teach you always to put God first in your lives.

  DEUTERONOMY 14:23b (TLB)

  Honor the Lord by giving him the first part of all your income, and he will fill your barns [to overflowing!]

  PROVERBS 3:9–10 (TLB)

- **I must _____ and _____ for the future.**

  The wise man saves for the future, but the foolish man spends whatever he gets.

  PROVERBS 21:20 (TLB)

  Money that comes easily disappears quickly, but money that is gathered little by little will grow.

  PROVERBS 13:11 (NCV)

  Develop your business first before building your house.

  PROVERBS 24:27 (TLB)

- **I must set up a _____ to get myself out of debt.**

  Don't withhold repayment of your debts.

  PROVERBS 3:27 (TLB)

  Let no debt remain outstanding.

  ROMANS 13:8 (NIV)

159

- **I must _____ my spending.**

  Plan carefully and you will have plenty; if you act too quickly, you will never have enough.

  PROVERBS 21:5 (TEV)

  Stupid people spend their money as fast as they get it.

  PROVERBS 21:20b (TEV)

- I must _____ what I have.

Godliness with contentment is great gain.

1 TIMOTHY 6:6 (NIV)

It is better to be satisfied with what you have than to be always wanting something else.

ECCLESIASTES 6:9 (TEV)

Keep your life free from love of money, and be content with what you have, for [God] has said, "I will never leave you nor forsake you."

HEBREWS 13:5 (ESV)

"Don't worry . . . Your heavenly Father already knows perfectly well [what you need], and he will give [it] to you if you give him first place in your life and live as he wants you to."

MATTHEW 6:31–33 (TLB)

160

You have to decide if you are going to trust God or yourself with your finances. Are you going to do it your way or are you going to do it God's way?

◇ DISCOVERY QUESTIONS
(PICK AT LEAST ONE OR TWO)

- What difference does it make when you consider that **your money is on loan from God**?

- How might your financial habits change if you asked yourself every day, "**How does God want me to spend his money**?"

- Why do money issues cause so much stress in people's lives? What would life look like if we put our **trust in God instead of our finances**?

- Why do you think so many people find it hard to budget? What tools have you found helpful in "telling your money where it should go?"

◈ PUTTING IT INTO PRACTICE

Where do you want to be three months from now with your financial health? What is one thing you will do to take a step in that direction? Not one thing you **could** do, or **might** do, but one thing you **will** do. If you are married, be sure to talk with your spouse and come to an agreement on your financial goal. Review Rick's video outline to help you with ideas. Share your goal with one other person in your group.

Write your financial health goal in the space below.

MY THREE-MONTH FINANCIAL HEALTH **GOAL**

Now transfer your **Three-Month Financial Health Goal** to your **My Three-Month Goals** list on page vi.

◈ PRAYER DIRECTION

Pray for your group's prayer requests. Be sure to record their requests on the **Small Group Prayer and Praise Report** on page 218. Be sure to remember to pray for any financial needs that might have been expressed in your time together as a group.

◈ DIVING DEEPER
WANT TO GO DEEPER IN YOUR FINANCIAL HEALTH?

FOR YOU

- Read the **daily devotions** for days 36 to 42 in your workbook.

- Read the **Memory Verse** on page 157 every day this week as part of your quiet time. See if you can have it memorized before your next group meeting.

- Visit **www.saddleback.com** and check out all of the free online training and resources for your financial health.

FOR THE GROUP

Consider for your next group study *Managing Our Finances God's Way*. This seven-week, video-based small group study will inspire you to **live debt-free and to manage your finances** in a way that relieves your stress and glorifies God. Available at **www.saddlebackresources.com**.

MANAGING OUR FINANCES STUDY GUIDE

This study guide accompanies the Managing Our Finances DVD.

MANAGING OUR FINANCES DVD

A 7-week, video-based study that will inspire you to live debt-free and manage your finances in a way that enables you to respond to God's calling on your life.

SADDLEBACKRESOURCES.COM

TRANSFORMED IN MY FINANCIAL HEALTH
DAY 36

He who refreshes others will himself be refreshed.

PROVERBS 11:25 (NIV)

It pays to give.

There is a universal principle at work called "the law of sowing and reaping," and it is a spiritual reality. We see it in this passage in terms of "refreshment." You give some refreshment and you will be refreshed yourself. Give some relief to someone else and you will be relieved.

When I was a kid I worked one summer for a family that was pretty well-to-do. They would have parties out on the lake, and it was my job to walk around and serve appetizers and beverages to the guests. Five poor friends and I were living in a guest house on the property, and our usually meager meals were augmented every time there was a party and we were called upon to serve. I could have rewritten this verse for myself: "He who serves a few refreshments will get to eat a few refreshments himself!"

Later in life, with a somewhat fuller measure of maturity, I began to understand this idea in a deeper way. The Scripture explains, *"Whoever sows sparingly will also reap sparingly, and whoever sows generously will also reap generously"* (2 Corinthians 9:6 NIV).

When God sees generosity that flows from us to others, whether it be in time or money or love, he takes pleasure in us. In a generous heart God finds a portrait of himself. When we give like God gives, we become a reflection of his bountiful love for all of us. God rewards us as we give freely by freely giving back to each of us more than we could imagine.

Here's what this Scriptural promise means to me:

You want to be blessed? Bless others. You want to be greatly blessed? Bless others richly!

You want to be loved? Love. You want to be deeply loved? Love a lot!
You want to be prosperous? Give. You want to be very, very prosperous? Give a lot!

Remember this: *"Whoever sows sparingly will also reap sparingly, and whoever sows generously will also reap generously."* It's a fact of life. It's the truth. It pays to give.

What did you hear?

What do you think?

165

What will you do?

Now talk to God . . .

> *"So do not worry, saying, 'What shall we eat?' or 'What shall we drink?' or 'What shall we wear?' For the pagans run after all these things, and your heavenly Father knows that you need them. But seek first his kingdom and his righteousness, and all these things will be given to you as well."*

MATTHEW 6:31–33 (NIV)

Jesus' words about what we eat, drink and wear are so practical. He reminds us that behavior reflects belief. If you believe God is your Provider, you will behave that way, obeying him, serving others, and believing *"all these things will be given to you as well."* Your focus will be on the kingdom of God. But if you believe you are your own provider, you will behave that way, worrying and scrambling to make ends meet. Your focus will be on the kingdom of you.

166

Jesus contrasts attitudes and actions which are either earthbound (a pagan's) or eternal (a disciple's) life-investments. Some people's investment is earthbound: running from this to that, moving from relationship to relationship, job to job, hobby to sports to recreation, following fads, taking seminars and therapies, and purchasing the latest self-help books. They are often fiscally challenged, squandering money, and using people to try to get ahead. Unhappy and restless, they look for materialistic fulfillment in all the wrong places because Jesus Christ is not the center of their life. They look to themselves to supply their needs.

A Christ-follower's investment is eternal: following Jesus, *"seeking his kingdom and his righteousness,"* building relationships through loving God and serving others, finding meaning and purpose in their work, and regularly dialoguing with God through the Scriptures, worship, prayer, and by listening to the Holy Spirit. They are often fiscally healthy, using money to love God and people. They are satisfied, integrated and content because Jesus is the center of life. **They look to God to supply their needs.**

So stop stressing about food, drink, and clothes. Start *"seeking the kingdom of God and his righteousness,"* as the foundation for life-investing and your financial health.

What did you hear?

What do you think?

What will you do?

Now talk to God . . .

167

TRANSFORMED IN MY FINANCIAL HEALTH
DAY 38

"Bring the whole tithe into the storehouse, that there may be food in my house. Test me in this," says the Lord Almighty, "and see if I will not throw open the floodgates of heaven and pour out so much blessing that you will not have room enough for it."

MALACHI 3:10 (NIV)

There are three words in this verse you must understand to be financially whole: tithe, test and blessing. The word tithe means 10%. I don't know why God tells us to give 10%; he could have said 50% or 30% or 90%. I do know that what we give is an act of trust and worship. Jesus affirmed this in Matthew 23:23 as he taught that we should tithe. When the Father says it and Jesus affirms it, it's a no brainer that we are to do it.

God obviously knew this would be hard for us, so he said, *"Put me to the test."* This is the only place in all of Scripture where God tells us to put him to the test. He knows that as he shows himself to be faithful, our heart for giving will only increase.

To be financially healthy you also need to understand God's idea of blessing. A blessing is not a purchase, it is a gift. If you only give to God in order to get exactly what you want, you are thinking too small. You are cheating yourself out of all that God wants to give you. God does give material blessings on earth, no doubt. But beyond that, he gives the blessings of being able to give to others, of growth and change in your own life, and of investing your life now in ways that make a difference for eternity. God's blessings will not always be what you expect, they will be more than you could have imagined.

168

What did you hear?

What do you think?

What will you do?

Now talk to God . . .

TRANSFORMED IN MY FINANCIAL HEALTH
DAY 39

*Honor the Lord with your wealth, with the firstfruits of all
your crops; then your barns will be filled to overflowing,
and your vats will brim over with new wine.*

PROVERBS 3:9-10 (NIV)

**There are more verses in the Bible about giving and tithing than any other
topic.** In fact over half of Jesus' parables deal with material possessions. Jesus spoke
more about money than he did about heaven or hell. Why? There are a number of
reasons why the Bible has so much to say about finances, but let's look at just two.

First, God wants you to become like him, and he is generous. God's generosity
flows out of his love for you and me. The most famous verse in the Bible, John 3:16, is
about God's generosity, *"God so loved the world that he **gave** his only Son . . ."*

Everything you have is because of God's great generosity and love. And he wants you
to honor him by giving back to him the "first part" of what you make. He blesses your
life so that you can be a blessing to others. Generosity breaks the grip of greed and
materialism on your life. A loving heart is a generous heart, and you are most like Jesus
when you give.

Second, God wants you to trust him with your finances. Money tends to
dominate our lives. So much of our time is spent making it, spending it, saving it,
investing it, or giving it. Financial tensions and conflicts are still one of the top five
reasons for divorce. God's money management plan is simple: trust him with your
wealth by giving to him first, *"then your barns will be filled to overflowing, and your
vats will brim with new wine."* In other words, trust God with your finances and he
will meet your needs.

In a world of economic uncertainty, God's plan for your finances is the best investment
you can make for your future. Ask God to help you overcome any fear or worry you
might have about trusting him and becoming more generous with your finances.

DAILY DEVOTIONS: DAY 39

What did you hear?

What do you think?

What will you do?

171

Now talk to God . . .

TRANSFORMED IN MY FINANCIAL HEALTH
DAY 40

Keep your lives free from the love of money and be content with what you have, because God has said, "Never will I leave you; never will I forsake you."

HEBREWS 13:5 (NIV)

What does it mean to love money? It means worshiping money, and worshiping money is a problem. The Bible makes it clear we are to worship God alone. When you worship something, you give your time, your resources and your energy to that thing. Whatever you worship consumes your life. How can we avoid worshiping money? What would it look like to have money, use money and make money without worshiping it? **The answer is contentment.**

What is contentment? Contentment is not saying, "I like where I'm at," as though you should never have any financial goals or you should not try to increase your net worth. In fact, God says, *"Those who work hard will prosper"* (Proverbs 13:4 NLT). Contentment is saying, **"Regardless of my circumstances, I have Christ in my life."** That's contentment. Contentment isn't based on your financial status. Rather, it is based on your relationship with God. We are content because God has promised that no matter what, he is with us and he will never forsake us. So, I can be content in my present circumstances because my contentment is not based upon them.

If you are searching for contentment, look beyond your present circumstances. Look beyond the here and now. Look to the promise of God. Have eternal perspective. God says he will always be with you. You have eternal life in him. As a result, you can be content in whatever current financial circumstances you find yourself. Whether you are materially rich or not, you are rich in God.

172

What did you hear?

_____
_____
_____
_____
_____

What do you think?

_____
_____
_____
_____
_____

What will you do?

_____
_____
_____
_____

Now talk to God . . .

_____
_____
_____
_____
_____

TRANSFORMED IN MY FINANCIAL HEALTH
DAY 41

And God is able to bless you abundantly, so that in all things at all times, having all that you need, you will abound in every good work.

2 CORINTHIANS 9:8 (NIV)

You are blessed to be a blessing. You're not meant to just sit back and bask in God's grace. Grace is given so that you can abound in good works. We're saved by grace. We're forgiven by grace. The Bible says we're strengthened by grace. We're set free from problems and sins by grace. All of the talents you have were given to you as a gift of grace. You're used by God's grace. The Bible says we're kept saved by God's grace. You're transformed by grace.

Robert Louis Stevenson said, "There is nothing in the universe but God's grace." We walk upon it, we breathe it, we live and die by it. God's grace is what holds everything together. If it weren't for God's grace, your life would fall apart, your family would fall apart, this nation would fall apart, the world would stop spinning on its axis. It is all held together by God's grace. **Everything in life is a blessing from God.**

Knowing all that God has given us, how could we possibly just use it for ourselves? God's abundance is not an invitation to indulgence, it is a call to generosity. God blesses you so you can bless other people. And how do you bless others? By giving to them what God has given you: your skills, your time, your treasures, your talents. When you give out of what God has given to you, this verse says you are abounding in every good work. That is the richest life you could possibly live.

What did you hear?

_____
_____
_____
_____

What do you think?

_____
_____
_____
_____

What will you do?

_____
_____
_____
_____

Now talk to God . . .

_____
_____
_____
_____

TRANSFORMED IN MY FINANCIAL HEALTH
DAY 42

"Give, and it will be given to you. A good measure, pressed down, shaken together and running over, will be poured into your lap. For with the measure you use, it will be measured to you.

LUKE 6:38 (NIV)

The picture in this verse comes from a man going to get seed from an open air market. The owner of the store says, "I'll sell you a basket worth of seed for so much money." So he pours the seed in, and then he shakes it and presses it so that he can get the most seed in his basket.

That's the way God gives. You give to him, he gives back. You shake it up and he gives more until it's just overflowing. Our God is a generous God! When you realize God's generosity, you lose your fear of planting the seed he has given you. Fear causes us to hold on to what we have, but faith gives us the courage to depend on God and plant seeds.

When you have a need, plant a seed. Seed is precious, but it is absolutely worthless until you spread it around. Imagine two farmers. One says, "I've got all this seed. I think I'll just hoard it this year. I want to protect it." The other farmer says, "No, I'm going to take all I the seed I have and spread it all over my field." At the harvest nine months later you see the difference. One man is a tragedy. Not only does he not harvest anything, but that which he kept has probably rotted. But the man who sowed generously sees God bless him with a rich harvest.

The more you give, the more God gives to you. The more you use your talents, the more you use your time, the more you use your money for good, the more God can multiply it in your life. You release your faith through a practical action. Plant a seed today. **Make a deposit. Act in faith. Step out.**

What did you hear?

_____
_____
_____
_____
_____

What do you think?

_____
_____
_____
_____
_____

What will you do?

_____
_____
_____
_____
_____

Now talk to God . . .

_____
_____
_____
_____
_____

177

NOTES

NOTES

179

Origami
butterfly

1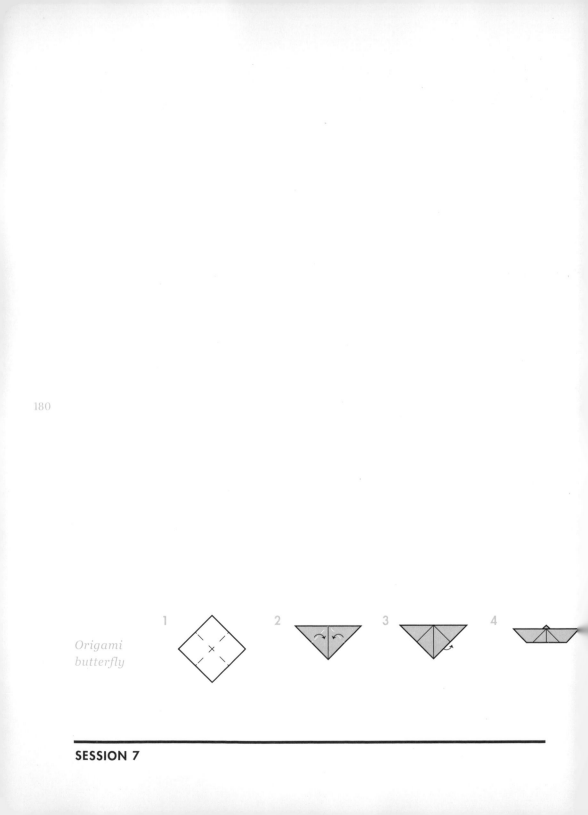

2

3

4

SESSION 7

TRANSFORMED IN MY VOCATIONAL HEALTH

SESSION 7

WEEKEND SERMON NOTES

SESSION 7

SESSION 7
TRANSFORMED IN MY VOCATIONAL HEALTH

◇ CHECKING IN

- Which of the seven financial health principles from your devotional reading this past week was **the most meaningful to you**?

- If you could have any job in the world, what would it be and why?

◈ MEMORY VERSE

Whatever you do, work at it with all your heart, as working for the Lord, not for men.

COLOSSIANS 3:23 (NIV)

185

◇ WATCH THE VIDEO LESSON NOW AND FOLLOW ALONG IN YOUR OUTLINE.

→

◈ TRANSFORMED IN MY VOCATIONAL HEALTH

"What profit is it to a man if he gains the whole world, and loses his own soul?"

MATTHEW 16:26 (NKJV)

SEVEN BIBLICAL ATTITUDES **FOR A HEALTHY WORK LIFE**

- **I must start working _____ wherever I am.**

  Whatever you do, work at it with all your heart.

  COLOSSIANS 3:23 (NIV)

- **This job is a _____ from God.**

  "Whoever can be trusted with very little can also be trusted with much . . . If you have not been trustworthy with someone else's property, who will give you property of your own?"

  LUKE 16:10–12 (NIV)

- **God is _____ .**

  Work hard so God can say to you, "Well done." Be a good workman, one who does not need to be ashamed when God examines your work.

  2 TIMOTHY 2:15 (TLB)

- **My _____ determines my _____ .**

  The diligent find freedom in their work; the lazy are oppressed by work.

  PROVERBS 12:24 (MSG)

186

Never be lazy in your work, but serve the Lord enthusiastically.

ROMANS 12:11 (TLB)

- **I must understand who I'm really** _____ .

    Work hard and cheerfully at whatever you do, as though you were working for the Lord rather than for people. Remember that the Lord will give you an inheritance as your reward, and the Master you are serving is Christ.

COLOSSIANS 3:23–24 (NLT)

- **I must concentrate on building** _____ .

- **I must care about** _____ .

    Whatever you do, do it with kindness and love.

1 CORINTHIANS 16:14 (TLB)

    Don't be concerned only about your own interests, but also be concerned about the interests of others.

PHILIPPIANS 2:4 (GWT)

    Always be humble and gentle. Be patient with each other, making allowance for each other's faults because of your love.

EPHESIANS 4:2 (NLT)

- **I must exceed what is** _____ .

    Servants, do what you're told by your earthly masters. And don't just do the minimum that will get you by. Do your best.

COLOSSIANS 3:22 (MSG)

    "If anyone requires you to go one mile, go two miles with him."

MATTHEW 5:41 (NJB)

187

- **I must expand my skills with** _____ .

> *If the ax is dull and its edge unsharpened, more strength is needed but skill will bring success.*

- **I must dedicate my work to be used for** _____ .

> *Commit your work to the Lord, and then your plans will succeed.*

PROVERBS 16:3 (NLT)

We are Christ's ambassadors.

2 CORINTHIANS 5:20 (NLT)

188

◇ DISCOVERY QUESTIONS
(PICK AT LEAST ONE OR TWO)

- What does it look like for you to live for the glory of God in your workplace? What are some practical ways you can **turn your work into an act of worship**?

- Think of one person you know who could use some **encouragement** in their work this week. What can you do to help them?

- The Bible says, *"We are Christ's ambassadors"* (2 Corinthians 5:20 NLT). What does an ambassador do? Whose interests does an ambassador represent? How can you be Christ's ambassador in your workplace?

- How many of the things that are frustrating you at work right now would be no big deal if you chose to **see God as your boss**? What is one thing you think would change in your perspective and attitude towards your work?

◈ PUTTING IT INTO PRACTICE

Where do you want to be three months from now with your vocational health? What is one thing you will do to take a step in that direction? Not one thing you **could** do, or **might** do, but one thing you **will** do. Review Rick's video outline to help you with ideas. Share your goal with one other person in your group.

Write your vocational health goal in the space below.

MY THREE-MONTH VOCATIONAL HEALTH **GOAL**

Now transfer your **Three-Month Vocational Health Goal** to your **My Three-Month Goals** list on pages vi to vii.

◈ PRAYER DIRECTION

Spend some time praying for each other's workplaces and the roles each of you plays in that setting.

If there are any prayer requests related to work, add them to the **Small Group Prayer and Praise Report** on page 218.

◈ DIVING DEEPER
WANT TO GO DEEPER IN YOUR VOCATIONAL HEALTH?

FOR YOU

- Read the **daily devotions** for days 43 to 49 in your workbook.

- Read the **Memory Verse** on page 185 every day this week as part of your quiet time. See if you can have it memorized before your next group meeting.

- Visit **www.saddleback.com** and check out all of the free online vocational training and resources to help you in your work life. Sign up for the **"Weekly Workplace Wisdom" eNewsletter. "Weekly Workplace Wisdom"** is our free devotional for working individuals to help you apply your faith at work. Every Tuesday we post to our blog a biblical perspective on a situation you may be facing at work, such as getting energized for work, resolving conflict, listening, building relationships, and the purpose of work.

FOR THE GROUP

Consider for your next group study *Christians in the Workplace*. This six-session, video-based small group study gives you a biblical perspective of the role God wants you to play wherever you work. Available at **www.saddleback.com**.

Pastor Rick would love to hear how this study has impacted your life. Please write to him at **pastorrick@saddleback.com**

CHRISTIANS IN THE WORKPLACE

This study has been carefully designed to energize and equip you to follow Christ as you fulfill your job description. Each lesson offers you the opportunity to transform the way you perform your work every day.

CHRISTIANS IN THE WORKPLACE DVD

Six sessions on how to follow Christ as you fulfill your job description.

SADDLEBACKRESOURCES.COM

193

*Commit your work to the Lord, and then your plans
will succeed.*

PROVERBS 16:3 (NLT)

There comes a point of decision where you have to stop talking and start acting. You have to begin. Once you've decided a risk is worth taking, you take off. You can't get to second base without leaving first.

Think of a trapeze artist. There is that moment of truth where she swings out to catch the bar that is swinging towards her. But in order to reach the bar, she has to let go of the one she is swinging on. If she doesn't let go, she just swings back to where she started. But if she does let go, there's a split second in time where she is hanging in mid-air, thirty feet above the ground, and holding on to absolutely nothing. That's what faith looks like.

Commit your work to the Lord, and then your plans will succeed. First you commit your goal to God, then you make your plans, then you take a step of faith, confident that God will give you success. How do you know when you've committed your plans or work or business to the Lord? He gets to be involved in the decisions. That means you pray about every decision. Planning without prayer is presumption. It also means that you make decisions that fit with the truth of his Word. You worship at work by obeying God. And when you find success, you give God the glory. **There is no limit to what God will do in the life of the person or the business that gives him the glory.**

What did you hear?

_____
_____
_____
_____
_____

What do you think?

_____
_____
_____
_____
_____

What will you do?

_____
_____
_____
_____
_____

195

Now talk to God . . .

_____
_____
_____
_____
_____

TRANSFORMED IN MY VOCATIONAL HEALTH
DAY 44

But remember the Lord your God, for it is he who gives you the ability to produce wealth.

DEUTERONOMY 8:18a (NIV)

Everything you have is a gift from God, including your ability to create wealth. After all, who gave you your hands and your brain? Who gave you your talents and abilities? You wouldn't have anything if it wasn't for the grace of God. You wouldn't even be alive.

This verse tells us that producing wealth is an ability. You might have great abilities in this area. Perhaps God has gifted you with a strong business sense and you are just naturally good at making money. That is a God-given ability. And since God gave it to you, you really can't be prideful about it. On the other hand, you might be a person who is always struggling financially. Don't be discouraged; ask God for the ability to produce what you need and remember that you have other abilities.

The great truth of this verse is that you can make money to the glory of God. If you have a beautiful voice, you should sing to the glory of God. If you have strong athletic skills, you should run to the glory of God. If you have a great business sense, you should make money to the glory of God. How can the business ability to make a deal, close a sale, plan a project—how in the world can that ability be used for the glory of God? By recognizing where that ability came from. By giving back to him the first ten percent of your income from the profits. By acting ethically and morally. And by providing a legitimate service or product that can help people. That all brings glory to God.

Why did God give you the ability to create wealth? It's not just for yourself. God's abilities are given to us so that we can serve him and serve others. **Every ability is given by God and every ability can be used for God's glory.**

What did you hear?

_____

_____

_____

_____

_____

What do you think?

_____

_____

_____

_____

_____

What will you do?

_____

_____

_____

_____

_____

Now talk to God . . .

_____

_____

_____

_____

_____

TRANSFORMED IN MY VOCATIONAL HEALTH
DAY 45

Trust in the Lord with all your heart, and lean not on your own understanding; in all your ways acknowledge him, and he shall direct your paths.

PROVERBS 3:5–6 (NKJV)

It's our heart that often fails us.

As a pastor, I've been included in many a eulogy. I can remember hearing these words at the passing of a businessman and friend: "Because of the stress and pressures he faced in business, his heart failed him."

The hidden meaning behind these words was clear. His heart gave out, it failed or quit on him, because of stress, fear, and the concerns of what the world was throwing at him. He was such a brilliant and talented leader. Wealthy. Strategic. Visionary. And yet, all of his wisdom and understanding was not enough to lean on. I have a feeling that there was always a lingering question, "Am I getting it right?"

There will always be questions in our hearts and minds if we are leaning on our own understanding.

It's totally different when we rely wholly upon the wisdom of God and can clearly and unashamedly declare, "I am NOT a self-made man. I lean on the Lord. It is clearly God who has gotten me this far. Without him, I would be lost trying to live life on my own."

As God's people, we can always depend upon him. It's when we are not leaning wholly upon him and we start trusting ourselves that we begin to second guess our own decisions. We wonder, we lack confidence, we worry, fret and stress out . . . and our hearts can fail us.

So, starting today, meet with God every morning in prayer, consult his Word for direction, and commit yourself to live the life that God would have you live. He will lead you, guide you, and set your paths straight. **You have his word on it.**

What did you hear?

_____
_____
_____
_____
_____
_____

What do you think?

_____
_____
_____
_____
_____
_____

What will you do?

_____
_____
_____
_____
_____

Now talk to God . . .

_____
_____
_____
_____
_____

199

TRANSFORMED IN MY VOCATIONAL HEALTH
DAY 46

For the Lord grants wisdom! From his mouth come knowledge and understanding. He grants a treasure of common sense to the honest. He is a shield to those who walk with integrity.

PROVERBS 2:6–7 (NLT)

Some people are good with words, but God is better. He can do much more with words than any man. He created the world by speaking it into being. You exist because he spoke.

Since the Bible is God's Word, a verse from the Bible is much more powerful than a wishful line inside a fortune cookie. A verse is what God says, recorded in ink. When we read it, the Holy Spirit makes it alive in us. He said it, you receive it.

Today's verse is just four lines long, but each line is powerful:

The first line describes the gift God gives. He gives wisdom. He grants it. Now that's a grant you want to apply for. We all want wisdom, especially in the workplace.

The second line tells you where the wisdom comes from: it's his words. Everything he says is wise. He is the wisest person in the universe. Listening to him makes you wise.

The third line uncovers the mystery of who receives wisdom. It's those who are honest. In fact, he gives them a treasury of common sense. Have you noticed that common sense isn't very common?

The fourth line tells you who keeps this wisdom. After all, you don't want to lose it. In one sentence, he tells you that he protects you and your wisdom when you walk in integrity.

So God has wisdom. He is the source. He gives it to the honest. He protects it in those with integrity. There you have it, the formula to finding, gaining and keeping wisdom.

What did you hear?

_____
_____
_____
_____
_____

What do you think?

_____
_____
_____
_____
_____

What will you do?

_____
_____
_____
_____
_____

Now talk to God . . .

_____
_____
_____
_____
_____

TRANSFORMED IN MY VOCATIONAL HEALTH
DAY 47

Plans fail for lack of counsel, but with many advisers they succeed.

PROVERBS 15:22 (NIV)

This truth applies to your personal life and your work life. Like most people, there are probably some things you are good at, and some things that you need to improve on. Also like most people, you're probably more keenly aware of the weaknesses in your life than you are of the strengths you have. That's why so many New Year's resolutions are made every December 31st. **We all want to improve.**

But how?

There are two main ways we can sharpen our skills and shore up our weaknesses. There's the hard way, and the easy way. The hard way is by trial and error. This is the painful way that makes us feel like we have to learn everything by experience. We have to make all the mistakes. We feel the need to do it all on our own.

The easy way is to learn from other people. We learn from their mistakes, and we listen to their advice. Who do you have in your life to turn to for counsel? Look around your small group, look for people you admire, people who love Jesus and who can help you. This way requires that you ask for help, that you seek *"many advisers."* Having people come alongside you and offer help and counsel means that you don't have to carry the burden on your own. You have the shared wisdom of many people to help you solve problems and reach your goals.

As you think about your challenges, or your weaknesses, or the areas you'd like to improve, ask yourself, **"Am I trying to do it all on my own?"** If the answer is yes, take a few minutes to write down the names of a few people you can ask for wise counsel. Then, pick up the phone and call them. You'll be one step closer to success.

What did you hear?

What do you think?

What will you do?

203

Now talk to God . . .

> *Consider it pure joy, my brothers and sisters, whenever you*
> *face trials of many kinds, because you know that the testing*
> *of your faith produces perseverance.*

JAMES 1:2–3 (NIV)

People are like tea bags. You don't know what's inside of them until you put them in hot water. Stress and problems have the uncanny ability to reveal what's inside each of us.

God says to, *"Consider it pure joy, whenever you face trials."* The word "consider" tells us that we have a choice. We can't choose our trials but we can always choose how we respond. So how does God want us to respond to these trials? He wants us to consider it joy. In fact, "pure joy!"

Author and speaker Kay Warren says, "Joy is the settled assurance that God is in control of all the details of my life, the quiet confidence that ultimately everything is going to be alright, and the determined choice to praise God in all things."

When we choose to face our trials with joy, the Bible says the test of our faith produces perseverance.

Notice that James says, *"When* [not if] *you face trials . . ."* Storms in life are inevitable. If you're not in a storm right now, just wait—you will encounter one soon enough. Nobody sails through life easily from the cradle to the grave. What's most important is how you choose to face your storms.

If you allow it, God will use storms to work off the rough edges of your personality, to help you regain perspective of who and what is most important, and to grow you up to spiritual maturity.

So the next time you find yourself in a storm, choose to focus on God and not your problem. Consider that there might be something even greater at work in your life than just the trial you are facing. And decide daily to choose joy in spite of your circumstances.

What did you hear?

What do you think?

What will you do?

Now talk to God . . .

> *Whatever you do, work at it with all your heart, as working for the Lord, not for men, since you know that you will receive an inheritance from the Lord as a reward. It is the Lord Christ you are serving.*

COLOSSIANS 3:23–24 (NIV)

You might file receipts for no other reason than to keep your job. You may fetch coffee out of duty, make small talk out of courtesy, or visit potential clients for the profit. On any given workday, you do more activities than you're aware of, for more reasons than you can count.

You do certain tasks on autopilot; others feel like chores. But then there are tasks you feel you were made to do . . . and maybe you were.

206 This verse changes everything by telling us that whatever the task, we should do it for more than just the reason at hand. We could jokingly say that we must work with "a double motive": to get things done **and** to work for Christ. The latter is most important.

Every dull task changes when done for your Creator. He is the one you love. He is the one who loves you. This mutual love puts you to work. It compels you to make every effort to turn your activities into gifts for him.

Yes, you can serve Christ by processing lifeless receipts, by handing out coffee, by listening to colleagues, and by selling your clients what they need. But the secret sauce is your "double motive."

We don't deserve a reward for all of this. After all, we act out of love for Christ, and he gave us this love to begin with. But in the verse, he baffles us. He rewards us for every small thing. He serves his servants. **Now that's true love.**

What did you hear?

What do you think?

What will you do?

Now talk to God . . .

RESOURCES

HELPS FOR HOSTS
TOP TEN IDEAS FOR NEW HOSTS

CONGRATULATIONS! As the host of your small group, you have responded to the call to help shepherd Jesus' flock. Few other tasks in the family of God surpass the contribution you will be making. As you prepare to facilitate your group, whether it is one session or the entire series, here are a few thoughts to keep in mind.

Remember you are not alone. God knows everything about you, and he knew you would be asked to facilitate your group. Even though you may not feel ready, this is common for all good hosts. God promises, *"I will never leave you; I will never abandon you"* (Hebrews 13:5 TEV). Whether you are facilitating for one evening, several weeks, or a lifetime, you will be blessed as you serve.

1. **Don't try to do it alone.** Pray right now for God to help you build a healthy team. If you can enlist a co-host to help you shepherd the group, you will find your experience much richer. This is your chance to involve as many people as you can in building a healthy group. All you have to do is ask people to help. You'll be surprised at the response.

2. **Be friendly and be yourself.** God wants to use your unique gifts and temperament. Be sure to greet people at the door with a big smile . . . this can set the mood for the whole gathering. Remember, they are taking as big a step to show up at your house as you are to host a small group! Don't try to do things exactly like another host; do them in a way that fits you. Admit when you don't have an answer and apologize when you make a mistake. Your group will love you for it and you'll sleep better at night.

3. **Prepare for your meeting ahead of time.** Preview the session and write down your responses to each question.

4. **Pray for your group members by name.** Before your group arrives, take a few moments to pray for each member by name. You may want to review the **Small Group Prayer and Praise Report** at least once a week. Ask God to use your time together to touch the heart of each person in your group. Expect God to lead you to whomever he wants you to encourage or challenge in a special way. If you listen, God will surely lead.

5. **When you ask a question, be patient.** Someone will eventually respond. Sometimes people need a moment or two of silence to think about the question. If silence

doesn't bother you, it won't bother anyone else. After someone responds, affirm the response with a simple "thanks" or "great answer." Then ask, "How about somebody else?" or "Would someone who hasn't shared like to add anything?" Be sensitive to new people or reluctant members who aren't ready to say, pray, or do anything. If you give them a safe setting, they will blossom over time. If someone in your group is a wallflower who sits silently through every session, consider talking to them privately and encouraging them to participate. Let them know how important they are to you—that they are loved and appreciated, and that the group would value their input. Remember, still water often runs deep.

6. **Provide transitions between questions.** Ask if anyone would like to read the paragraph or Bible passage. Don't call on anyone, but ask for a volunteer, and then be patient until someone begins. Be sure to thank the person who reads aloud.

7. **Break into smaller groups occasionally.** With a greater opportunity to talk in a small circle, people will connect more with the study, apply more quickly what they're learning, and ultimately get more out of their small group experience. A small circle also encourages a quiet person to participate and tends to minimize the effects of a more vocal or dominant member.

8. **Small circles are also helpful during prayer time.** People who are unaccustomed to praying aloud will feel more comfortable trying it with just two or three others. Also, prayer requests won't take as much time, so circles will have more time to actually pray. When you gather back with the whole group, you can have one person from each circle briefly update everyone on the prayer requests from their subgroups. The other great aspect of subgrouping is that it fosters leadership development. As you ask people in the group to facilitate discussion or to lead a prayer circle, it gives them a small leadership step that can build their confidence.

9. **Rotate facilitators occasionally.** You may be perfectly capable of hosting each time, but you will help others grow in their faith and gifts if you give them opportunities to host the group.

10. **One final challenge (for new or first-time hosts).** Before your first opportunity to lead, look up each of the six passages listed below. Read each one as a devotional exercise to help prepare you with a shepherd's heart. Trust us on this one. If you do this, you will be more than ready for your first meeting.

When Jesus saw the crowds, he had compassion on them, because they were harassed and helpless, like sheep without a shepherd. ³⁷Then he said to his disciples, "The harvest is plentiful but the workers are few. ³⁸Ask the Lord of the harvest, therefore, to send out workers into his harvest field."

I am the good shepherd; I know my sheep and my sheep know me—¹⁵just as the Father knows me and I know the Father—and I lay down my life for the sheep.

Be shepherds of God's flock that is under your care, serving as overseers—not because you must, but because you are willing, as God wants you to be; ³not greedy for money, but eager to serve; not lording it over those entrusted to you, but being examples to the flock. ⁴And when the Chief Shepherd appears, you will receive the crown of glory that will never fade away.

212

If you have any encouragement from being united with Christ, if any comfort from his love, if any fellowship with the Spirit, if any tenderness and compassion, ²then make my joy complete by being like-minded, having the same love, being one in spirit and purpose. ³Do nothing out of selfish ambition or vain conceit, but in humility consider others better than yourselves. ⁴Each of you should look not only to your own interests, but also to the interests of others. ⁵Your attitude should be the same as that of Christ Jesus.

Let us hold unswervingly to the hope we profess, for he who promised is faithful. ²⁴And let us consider how we may spur one another on toward love and good deeds. ²⁵Let us not give up meeting together, as some are in the habit of doing, but let us encourage one another—and all the more as you see the Day approaching.

. . . but we were gentle among you, like a mother caring for her little children. ⁸We loved you so much that we were delighted to share with you not only the gospel of God but our lives as well, because you had become so dear to us. . . . ¹¹For you know that we dealt with each of you as a father deals with his own children, ¹²encouraging, comforting and urging you to live lives worthy of God, who calls you into his kingdom and glory.

FREQUENTLY ASKED QUESTIONS

HOW LONG WILL THIS GROUP MEET?

This study is seven sessions long. We encourage your group to add an eighth
session for a celebration. In your final session, each group member may decide
if he or she desires to continue on for another study. At that time you may also want to
do some informal evaluation, discuss your **Small Group Guidelines** (see page 204),
and decide which study you want to do next. We recommend you visit our Website at
www.saddlebackresources.com for more video-based small-group studies.

WHO IS THE HOST?

The host is the person who coordinates and facilitates your group meetings. In addition
to a host, we encourage you to select one or more group members to lead your group dis-
cussions. Several other responsibilities can be rotated, including refreshments, prayer
requests, worship, or keeping up with those who miss a meeting. Shared ownership in
the group helps everybody grow.

WHERE DO WE FIND NEW GROUP MEMBERS?

Recruiting new members can be a challenge for groups, especially new groups with
just a few people, or existing groups that lose a few people along the way. We encourage
you to use the **Circles of Life** diagram on page 203 of this study guide to brainstorm
a list of people from your workplace, church, school, neighborhood, family, and so on.
Then pray for the people on each member's list. Allow each member to invite several
people from their list. Some groups fear that newcomers will interrupt the intimacy
that members have built over time. However, groups that welcome newcomers generally
gain strength with the infusion of new blood. Remember, the next person you add
just might become a friend for eternity. Logistically, groups find different ways to add
members. Some groups remain permanently open, while others choose to open peri-
odically, such as at the beginning or end of a study. If your group becomes too large for
easy, face-to-face conversations, you can subgroup, forming a second discussion group
in another room.

HOW DO WE HANDLE THE CHILD-CARE NEEDS IN OUR GROUP?

Child-care needs must be handled very carefully. This is a sensitive issue. We suggest you seek creative solutions as a group. One common solution is to have the adults meet in the living room and share the cost of a baby sitter (or two) who can be with the kids in another part of the house. Another popular option is to have one home for the kids and a second home (close by) for the adults. If desired, the adults could rotate the responsibility of providing a lesson for the kids. This last option is great with school-age kids and can be a huge blessing to families.

CIRCLES OF LIFE
SMALL GROUP CONNECTIONS

DISCOVER WHO YOU CAN CONNECT IN COMMUNITY

Use this chart to help carry out one of the values in the **Group Guidelines**, to "Welcome Newcomers."

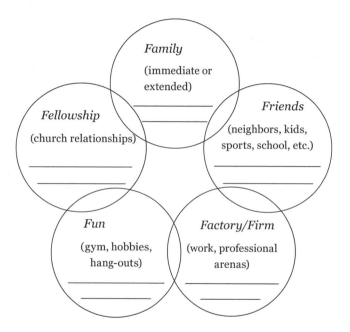

FOLLOW THIS SIMPLE THREE-STEP PROCESS:

1. List one to two people in each circle.

2. Prayerfully select one person or couple from your list and tell your group about them.

3. Give them a call and invite them to your next meeting. Over fifty percent of those invited to a small group say, "Yes!"

SMALL GROUP GUIDELINES

It's a good idea for every group to put words to their shared values, expectations, and commitments. Such guidelines will help you avoid unspoken agendas and unmet expectations. We recommend you discuss your guidelines during Session 1 in order to lay the foundation for a healthy group experience. Feel free to modify anything that does not work for your group.

WE AGREE TO THE FOLLOWING VALUES:

CLEAR PURPOSE — To grow healthy spiritual lives by building a healthy small group community

GROUP ATTENDANCE — To give priority to the group meeting (call if I am absent or late)

SAFE ENVIRONMENT — To create a safe place where people can be heard and feel loved (no quick answers, snap judgments, or simple fixes)

BE CONFIDENTIAL — To keep anything that is shared strictly confidential and within the group

CONFLICT RESOLUTION — To avoid gossip and to immediately resolve any concerns by following the principles of Matthew 18:15–17

SPIRITUAL HEALTH — To give group members permission to speak into my life and help me live a healthy, balanced spiritual life that is pleasing to God

LIMIT OUR FREEDOM — To limit our freedom by not serving or consuming alcohol during small group meetings or events so as to avoid causing a weaker brother or sister to stumble (1 Corinthians 8:1–13; Romans 14:19–21)

WELCOME NEWCOMERS — To invite friends who might benefit from this study and warmly welcome newcomers

BUILDING RELATIONSHIPS — To get to know the other members of the group and pray for them regularly

OTHER
_____

_____

_____

_____

We have also discussed and agree on the following items:

CHILD CARE _____

STARTING TIME _____

ENDING TIME _____

If you haven't already done so, take a few minutes to fill out the **Small Group Calendar** on page 207.

SMALL GROUP PRAYER AND PRAISE REPORT

This is a place where you can write each other's requests for prayer. You can also make a note when God answers a prayer. Pray for each other's requests. If you're new to group prayer, it's okay to pray silently or to pray by using just one sentence:

"God, please help _____ to _____."

DATE	PERSON	PRAYER REQUEST	PRAISE REPORT

SMALL GROUP CALENDAR

Healthy groups share responsibilities and group ownership. It might take some time for this to develop. Shared ownership ensures that responsibility for the group doesn't fall to one person. Use the calendar to keep track of social events, mission projects, birthdays, or days off. Complete this calendar at your first or second meeting. Planning ahead will increase attendance and shared ownership.

DATE	LESSON	LOCATION	FACILITATOR	SNACK OR MEAL
	Session 1			
	Session 2			
	Session 3			
	Session 4			
	Session 5			
	Session 6			
	Session 7			

PURPOSE DRIVEN
SPIRITUAL HEALTH ASSESSMENT

Test yourselves to make sure you are solid in the faith. Don't drift along taking everything for granted. Give yourselves regular checkups . . . Test it out. If you fail the test, do something about it.

2 CORINTHIANS 13:5 (MSG)

In Day 39 of The Purpose Driven Life, Rick Warren introduces the concept of a spiritual health assessment. He says that to maintain our physical health, we need regular check-ups with a doctor who can assess our vital signs—blood pressure, temperature, weight, and so on. For our spiritual health we need to regularly check and balance the five vital signs of a healthy Christian life:

Worship: You were planned for God's pleasure.
Fellowship: You were formed for God's family.
Discipleship: You were created to become like Christ.
Ministry: You were shaped for serving God.
Evangelism: You were made for a mission.

The Spiritual Health Assessment and Spiritual Health Planner measures your health at a particular point in time. It is not a tool to see how you measure up against other people; nor is it a tool to see how close you are to perfection. We all know we'll never be perfect this side of heaven. Rather, this is a tool that will help you evaluate your spiritual health, and give you direction for developing a plan to bring God's five purposes for your life into balance.

SPIRITUAL HEALTH ASSESSMENT

	Doesn't Match	Partial Match	Strong Match

WORSHIP: YOU WERE PLANNED FOR GOD'S PLEASURE

How I live my life shows that God is my highest priority 0 1 2 3 4 5

I am dependent on God for every aspect of my life 0 1 2 3 4 5

There is nothing in my life that I have not surrendered to (kept back from) God 0 1 2 3 4 5

I regularly meditate on God's Word and invite Him into my everyday activities 0 1 2 3 4 5

I have a deep desire to spend time in God's presence 0 1 2 3 4 5

I am the same person in public that I am in private 0 1 2 3 4 5

I have an overwhelming sense of God's awesomeness even when

I do not feel His presence 0 1 2 3 4 5

WORSHIP **TOTAL** _____

FELLOWSHIP: YOU WERE FORMED FOR GOD'S FAMILY

I am genuinely open and honest about who I am 0 1 2 3 4 5

I regularly use my time and resources to care for the needs of others 0 1 2 3 4 5

I have a deep and meaningful connection with others in the church 0 1 2 3 4 5

I have an easy time receiving advice, encouragement, and correction from others 0 1 2 3 4 5

I gather regularly with a group of Christians for fellowship and accountability 0 1 2 3 4 5

There is nothing in my relationships that is currently unresolved 0 1 2 3 4 5

There is nothing in the way I talk or act concerning others that I would

not be willing to share with them in person 0 1 2 3 4 5

FELLOWSHIP **TOTAL** _____

DISCIPLESHIP: YOU WERE CREATED TO BECOME LIKE CHRIST

I am quick to confess anything in my character that does not look like Christ 0 1 2 3 4 5

A review of how I use my finances shows that I think more about God

and others than I do about myself 0 1 2 3 4 5

I allow God's Word to guide my thoughts and change my actions 0 1 2 3 4 5

I am able to praise God during difficult times and see them as opportunities to grow 0 1 2 3 4 5

I find I am making better choices to do what is right when I am tempted to do wrong 0 1 2 3 4 5

I have found that prayer has changed how I view and interact with the world 0 1 2 3 4 5

I am consistent in pursuing habits that are helping me model my life after Jesus 0 1 2 3 4 5

DISCIPLESHIP **TOTAL** _____

	Doesn't Match	Partial Match	Strong Match

MINISTRY: YOU WERE SHAPED FOR SERVING GOD

I regularly use my time to serve God 0 1 2 3 4 5

I am currently serving God with the gifts and passions he has given me 0 1 2 3 4 5

I regularly reflect on how my life can have an impact for the Kingdom of God 0 1 2 3 4 5

I enjoy meeting the needs of others without expecting anything in return 0 1 2 3 4 5

I often think about ways to use my God-given gifts and abilities to please God 0 1 2 3 4 5

Those closest to me would say my life is a reflection of giving more than receiving . . . 0 1 2 3 4 5

I see my painful experiences as opportunities to minister to others 0 1 2 3 4 5

MINISTRY **TOTAL** _____

EVANGELISM: YOU WERE MADE FOR A MISSION

I feel personal responsibility to share my faith with those who don't know Jesus 0 1 2 3 4 5

I look for opportunities to build relationships with those who don't know Jesus 0 1 2 3 4 5

I regularly pray for those who don't know Christ 0 1 2 3 4 5

I am confident in my ability to share my faith 0 1 2 3 4 5

My heart is full of passion to share the good news of the gospel with

those who have never heard it 0 1 2 3 4 5

I find that my relationship with Jesus comes up frequently in my

conversations with those who don't know him 0 1 2 3 4 5

I am open to going anywhere God calls me, in whatever capacity, to share my faith

EVANGELISM **TOTAL** _____

Transfer your scores to the Spiritual Health Plan on the next page.

I will share my plan with _____

who will be my spiritual partner to help me balance the five Biblical purposes in my life.

PURPOSES	PRACTICES	PARTNERSHIP	PROGRESS
What purposes are out of balance?	What do I need to do?	How will my spiritual partner help me in this purpose?	What progress have I made?
WORSHIP How I scored myself: _____ How my friend scored me: _____			
FELLOWSHIP How I scored myself: _____ How my friend scored me: _____			
DISCIPLESHIP How I scored myself: _____ How my friend scored me: _____			
MINISTRY How I scored myself: _____ How my friend scored me: _____			
EVANGELISM How I scored myself: _____ How my friend scored me: _____			

223

RESOURCES

ANSWER KEY

SESSION ONE

• I must <u>LOVE JESUS</u> supremely.

• Spiritual health is measured by <u>LOVE</u>.

• I must <u>MEET WITH HIM DAILY</u>.

• I must <u>STUDY</u> and <u>DO</u> his Word.

• I must <u>TITHE</u> my income.

• I must learn to <u>LOVE OTHER BELIEVERS</u>.

• Spiritual growth happens in <u>COMMUNITY</u>.

• I must <u>SERVE OTHERS UNSELFISHLY</u>.

• I must pass on the <u>GOOD NEWS</u>.

SESSION TWO

• My body is God's <u>PROPERTY</u>.

• God expects me to <u>MANAGE</u> my body.

• My body will be <u>RESURRECTED</u> after I die.

• My body is connected to the <u>BODY OF CHRIST</u>.

• The Holy Spirit <u>LIVES IN</u> my body.

• Jesus <u>BOUGHT MY BODY</u> on the cross.

SESSION THREE

• Don't believe everything you <u>THINK</u>.

• Guard your mind against <u>GARBAGE</u>.

• Never let up on <u>LEARNING</u>.

• Renew your mind daily with <u>GOD'S WORD</u>.

• Let God stretch your <u>IMAGINATION</u>.

• Test every thought.

• Helmet your head.

• Imagine great thoughts.

• Nourish a godly mind.

• Keep on learning.

SESSION FOUR

• <u>REVEAL</u> my <u>HURT</u>.

• <u>RELEASE</u> those who have <u>HURT ME</u>.

• Replace <u>OLD LIES</u> with <u>GOD'S TRUTHS</u>.

• <u>REFOCUS</u> on the <u>FUTURE</u>.

• <u>REACH OUT</u> to help <u>OTHERS</u>.

SESSION FIVE

• <u>CASUAL</u> friends are the result of <u>CIRCUMSTANCES</u>.

- <u>CLOSE</u> friends are the result of <u>CHOICES</u>.

- <u>LAZY</u> people

- <u>ANGRY</u> people

- <u>IMMORAL</u> people

- <u>GREEDY</u> people

- <u>UNBELIEVING</u> people

- <u>CHALLENGE</u> me mentally

- <u>SUPPORT</u> me emotionally

- <u>STRENGTHEN</u> me spiritually

- Get interested in <u>OTHER PEOPLE</u>

- Don't be a <u>CHRONIC COMPLAINER</u>

- Be a <u>GOOD LISTENER</u>

- Accept people <u>UNCONDITIONALLY</u>

- Help people <u>FEEL SIGNIFICANT</u>

- Be <u>SYMPATHETIC</u>

- Stick with them in <u>TOUGH TIMES</u>

- Share <u>CHRIST</u> with them

SESSION SIX

- I must trust God as my <u>SOURCE</u> and <u>SUPPLIER</u>.

- I must keep <u>GOOD RECORDS</u>.

- I must give the first <u>TEN PERCENT</u> back to God.

- I must <u>SAVE</u> and <u>INVEST</u> for the future.

- I must set up a <u>REPAYMENT PLAN</u> to get myself out of debt.

- I must <u>BUDGET</u> my spending.

- I must <u>ENJOY</u> what I have.

SESSION SEVEN

- I must start working <u>ENTHUSIASTICALLY</u> wherever I am.

- This job is a <u>TEST</u> from God.

- God is <u>WATCHING</u>.

- My <u>ATTITUDE</u> determines my <u>JOY</u>.

- I must understand who I'm really <u>WORKING FOR</u>.

- I must concentrate on building <u>MY CHARACTER</u>.

- I must care about <u>PEOPLE I WORK WITH</u>.

- I must exceed what is <u>EXPECTED OF ME</u>.

- I must expand my skills with <u>CONTINUAL LEARNING</u>.

- I must dedicate my work to be used for <u>GOD'S PURPOSES</u>.

225

RESOURCES